Advanced Praise for

M000189029

"No business owner wants to go to court. It takes us away from our passion and purpose. The truth is many businesses are susceptible. Alex and Louis' book helps us close this gap. You can't afford not to read this book."

—Kary Oberbrunner
WSJ and *USA Today* Bestselling Author and CEO of Igniting Souls and Blockchain Life

"This book is a must-read for any entrepreneur and executive. As a leader, you can't be constantly playing defense and reacting to the unexpected. This is a blueprint on how to be prepared, have peace of mind, and allow leaders to do what they do best, apply their expertise to building their business."

—John R. DiJulius III
Best Selling author of *The Customer Service Revolution*

"*The Lawsuit-Free Company* by Alex and Lou is a game-changer! It brilliantly lays out the CoverMySix® method, turning potential legal nightmares into proactive strategies for success. A must-read for every business leader serious about safeguarding their future!"

—Ben Laws
CEO, Co-Founder, Evexia Wealth and Evexia Accounting

"As a business owner, this well-crafted book made me aware of previously unknown litigious risks and their potential negative effect on my business. Alex and Louis have expertly and masterfully laid out the six most important litigants to any business while providing a step-by-step solution to mitigate those risks. Litigation is not an if but a when. This quick, easy-to-read book prepares every business owner on how to limit their future loss of time, money, and mental anguish!"

—Gary Klaben
President, Coyle Financial

"Litigation may be fun to watch in the movies, but it's the last thing I want to do as a business owner. This book is a concise roadmap for business owners, clarifying where litigation risks exist and how to address them. Alex and Lou present a straightforward approach to helping companies clean up messes before they occur."

—Laura Steinbrink
Managing Member, Emerald Built Environments

"I became a social entrepreneur to change the world and help people gain employable tech skills, not to argue or experience costly miscommunications. In their new book, *The Lawsuit-Free Company*, co-authors Louis J. Licata and Alex Gertsburg show business owners how to apply much-needed CoverMySix® solutions to ease their most painful headaches. Read it, employ it, and feel assured that you're gaining actionable information that will help you sleep at night."

—Mel McGee
CEO, We Can Code It

"Navigating the legal landscape in the automotive industry is no easy feat, and the potential risks and uncertainties can be daunting. After going through CoverMySix's litigation risk assessment, I can confidently say our dealerships are now better equipped to safeguard our business from potential legal challenges and government investigations."

—Michael Tucci
General Counsel, Auto Services Unlimited

"As a business owner it's apparent that the laws and regulations governing running a business have become increasingly more complex and challenging to manage, causing a reactionary approach to managing crisis. This approach is stressful and expensive but not unusual for business leaders. Finding trusted tools and resources to help us navigate ahead of potential blind spots is crucial to the health of our company and our sanity.

Alex and Lou are one of us, business owners, who understand our exposure along with the day-to-day challenges we have, *and* they are experienced legal advisors who have created a tool that clearly outlines a thorough approach to protecting us as we manage growing our businesses. With CoverMySix® and *The Lawsuit-Free Company*, you get a clear road map to reduce the risk ahead and can focus on the vision and execution of your business."

—Adam Fleischer
CEO, The Wine Spot

"Spending time and energy locked in a lawsuit is the least effective way to build a business and culture of caring individuals. This book really helps entrepreneurs navigate the minefield of legal challenges that await us as we aspire to realize our full human potential. Alex and Lou have a proven process in CoverMySix® to minimize legal risk and shore up the operating basis so you can be a focused leader."

—Ben Bebenroth
President/Founder, Spice Hospitality Group

"While business leaders strive to control many facets of their business, they often have a feeling of minimal control over those that are litigious. Finally, there is a resource to provide the knowledge and strategic blueprint to implement and gain control over that aspect of management. Endless kudos and recommendations for the principles and solutions shared in this book!"

—Jason Smith
Founder & CEO, C2P

THE
LAWSUIT-FREE
COMPANY

HOW TO USE THE COVERMYSIX® METHOD TO MINIMIZE RISK, INCREASE VALUE, AND PROTECT YOUR FREEDOM

THE
LAWSUIT-FREE
COMPANY

HOW TO USE THE
COVERMYSIX® METHOD TO
MINIMIZE RISK, INCREASE VALUE,
AND PROTECT YOUR FREEDOM

Alex Gertsburg, Esq, and Louis J. Licata, Esq.

ethos
collective

Printed in the United States of America

Published by Ethos Collective™

PO Box 43, Powell, OH 43065

www.ethoscollective.vip

LCCN: 2023917551
Paperback ISBN: 978-1-63680-214-5
Hardcover ISBN: 978-1-63680-215-2
e-book ISBN: 978-1-63680-216-9

Available in paperback, hardcover, and e-book.

Contents

READ THIS FIRST!

This is not legal advice.

Alex and Lou are experienced litigators and business attorneys practicing law for over half a century combined. Their vast experience in the legal field has enabled them to accumulate valuable knowledge and insights, which they categorized into the six buckets of risk and exposure in this book. But make no mistake: Alex and Lou are not your lawyers, and you must seek the advice of YOUR OWN legal counsel, licensed to practice in YOUR state, for specific legal advice relevant to YOUR circumstances.

Alex and Lou's legal practice is nationwide, but they have yet to litigate cases in all 50 states, including Alaska and Arizona. The book's content, lessons, and experiences focus on their expertise in Ohio courtrooms. Although Ohio business laws tend to be very similar to those applicable to most businesses in the United States, it is nonetheless absolutely critical that you consult your legal counsel to provide advice tailored to your specific needs and circumstances, especially if your business operates in a state other than Ohio. Although the principles discussed in this book are generally applicable, they do not constitute a one-size-fits-all solution.

This book presents the CoverMySix® system. It is intended to assist business owners and decision-makers in avoiding and minimizing risks associated with litigation and government investigations. While this system has proven effective for our clients, it cannot and does not guarantee that you will eliminate the risk of all lawsuits. Unfortunately, in our legal system, anyone can file a complaint and sue you for just $250.

The CoverMySix system, if properly implemented, will create a six-sided fort around you and your business to protect against extended or needless litigation. For instance, the five-step waterfall dispute resolution provision is usually enforceable in most jurisdictions and can help steer disputes into a conference room instead of a courtroom. However, it cannot prevent someone from filing a frivolous lawsuit against you. In that case, the system can serve as a weapon to help you exit the courtroom as quickly as possible.

There is no magic wand or guarantee within these pages. Even if you do everything right, there is still a chance that you may end up in court, and you may even lose. The purpose of this book is to set you up for success as best as we can.

Thank you.

Introduction

The Ugly Truth about Litigation

JOHN POURED HIS HEART, soul, and money into building a successful company. He created an excellent reputation with his customers and cared for his employees like they were family.

But then, one day, it all came crashing down. John walked into his office to find a summons sitting on top of the stack of papers on his desk, staring at him like an expectant child. Steadying his hand, he set down his coffee and opened the letter. "You have twenty-eight days to respond to the complaint or a default judgment against your company will be entered."

John fell into his chair and reread the summons. "These allegations are outrageous: gross negligence, fraud, and willful misconduct," he said aloud for anyone passing to hear. "The plaintiff is a frivolous litigant." John knew the litigant wanted to make him bleed. As he read the summons for a third time, he homed in that the litigant was asking the court to certify the case as a class action and was requesting triple damages, punitive damages, and attorney's fees.

John would be stuck in court for the next eighteen months, minimum.

And it was all public record. Soon, his phone started ringing off the hook. A reporter wanted a statement. The plaintiff's lawyer has already issued her statement to the media. Then, one of his regular customers came in and said she saw his picture on the news. She had a lot of questions.

This was a nightmare.

John was paralyzed, but he made two phone calls.

"You are in the litigation casino now," his lawyer said. "The longer you stay, the more you pay."

Though John was faultless, he wasn't along for the ride because the other side reasonably articulated a good-faith basis to state a claim. He was looking to spend $50,000 in the first two months alone and up to a million dollars if the case went to trial. Then, there would be appeals and public relations consultants to deal with.

John's second call was to his insurance agent. "Please tell me I have coverage for this!"

The response was disquieting: "I'll let you know." *Click.*

After the carrier investigated, John would receive a "reservation of rights" letter with some grant of coverage if he did not violate any of the exclusions.

Thankfully, John bought the right coverage at the right amount and with a low deductible. But even though he did, he would still face a long and painful battle unless the plaintiff took a quick settlement.

⤜⤛

In the lawsuit business, even if you stand entirely faultless, defending yourself can cost you tens or hundreds of thousands of dollars, as well as your business, reputation, and peace of mind.

This price tag escalates if the case goes to trial, as the costs of expert witnesses, document preparation, court fees, and innumerable other expenses add up rapidly. Even with an insurance policy, there is no guarantee it will cover all litigation costs.

> EVEN IF YOU STAND ENTIRELY FAULTLESS, DEFENDING YOURSELF CAN COST YOU TENS OR HUNDREDS OF THOUSANDS OF DOLLARS AND YOUR BUSINESS, REPUTATION, AND PEACE OF MIND.

But you are not powerless. You have options, and this book guides you through them.

What Court Feels Like

Litigation is stressful, time-consuming, distracting, public, and expensive, even when everything goes according to plan. As experienced litigators, we have seen the toll it takes on even the most robust and secure clients. Plaintiff lawyers play a strategic game of making lawsuits the most convoluted, expensive experiences for business owners. One of our clients once described litigation as being trapped in a taxi in a foreign country, with the driver taking the longest possible route without telling you about it. It is no wonder that small business owners cite legal issues as their most significant source of stress.[1]

Litigation costs are rising, and more people are pursuing legal careers due to the growing demand for legal services. As reported in an article by *Above the Law* in August

2023, "lawyer headcount is up 3.9 percent, but demand is down, leading to a decline in productivity to the tune of 4.1 percent."[2] The median costs to litigate a civil action, such as a contract dispute, employment matter, real property dispute, premises liability case, or auto suit, are between $50,000 and $118,000.[3]

The name of the game for a smart business is not litigation defense. It's litigation protection and avoidance.

While it's not a 100% guarantee, a proactive approach is the best strategy. If someone takes legal action, a quick settlement is the next best option, as litigation wastes time and energy that businesses could better spend on growth, stabilization, operational efficiency, and maintaining client and employee satisfaction.

Once you're in court, getting out is a challenge. Your outcome and the speed and expense of that outcome depend on your lawyer's ability to get four personalities to align perfectly and agree: you, your lawyer, the other party, and their lawyer. If the case advances beyond the initial pleading stage, judges, mediators, arbitrators, and juries are added to the equation. These individuals are fallible human beings with biases, moods, and baggage beyond your control. Avoid them if you can. Be proactive.

CoverMySix helps you avoid litigation. That is what this book teaches. Once you are in litigation, you have already lost.

ONCE YOU ARE IN LITIGATION, YOU HAVE ALREADY LOST.

Who Should Read This Book?

Traditionally, businesses have been reactive, neglecting legal matters until they become too late to solve proactively. This approach leads to spending countless hours and resources in lawyers' offices, attending depositions, mediations, pretrial conferences, and going to trial.

This book is for business owners, key executives, advisors, consultants, in-house lawyers, and attorneys who want to proactively avoid needless litigation and manage risk. CoverMySix is a method designed to investigate, categorize, and minimize risk in a company. In addition to helping businesses directly, it is also an invaluable framework for in-house lawyers and attorneys who want to provide a 360-degree, holistic, and proactive approach to reducing their business clients' risk.

How to Build a Six-Sided Fortress

Only six plaintiffs can sue a business: customers, vendors, employees, shareholders, the government, and competitors. With their combined fifty-eight years of business and litigation experience, Alex and Lou have never encountered a plaintiff who didn't fit into one of these six categories.[4]

This six-plaintiff universe is the foundation for the CoverMySix (CM6) system. It organizes all major legal risks into these plaintiff groups, identifies the claims they can bring, and then the defenses to those claims. To establish compliance, our team performs extensive research, analysis, drafting, template generation, and checklist formulation for our clients. That's how we build a six-sided fort that protects our clients from these plaintiffs. *This framework has worked for every kind of business or industry we've encountered, of every size, in every geographic area in the US because the same six plaintiffs exist with all of them.* We are still amazed that businesses hire their lawyers reactively, in a haphazard "wait till we're sued" way when the CM6 scaffolding is available to them to build their fort and keep them safe.

After completing audits for numerous clients, including nursing homes, software companies, cannabis companies, and travel companies, we trademarked "CoverMySix" and started building a separate company around this innovative solution. Today, CoverMySix is a holistic and technology-enabled system that companies in any industry and any state can apply. By following the steps in the book, you can substantially reduce your legal risk and protect yourself from needless litigation.

Doing business in the United States means that you are subject to thousands of statutes, rules, and regulations at federal, state, local, and administrative levels. It is totally unfeasible (if not impossible) to comply with every possible risk, so CoverMySix employs Pareto's Principle (the "80/20 Rule") to identify and minimize exposure. We focus on the 20% of the risks that pose the greatest threat to your business. Time and time again, this approach has worked effectively to keep our clients out of the courtroom and focused on building their vision, making money, serving their customers, and keeping their employees happy.

Let's Talk about Insurance

Before diving in, let's revisit that moment when John needed to make that second call to his insurance agent. There are plenty of excellent insurance agents that we know and respect. The truth is that they are not lawyers. They know insurance, how to sell it, and some of the broader types of risks that your company is likely to face. They simply cannot, however, offer the deep litigation-based analysis that seasoned attorneys who have spent decades in courtrooms and as in-house counsel advising CEOs and shareholders on how to avoid litigation can. They have not seen the jury verdicts, and they have not walked hand-in-hand with clients as they've gone through the exasperation, stress, public shaming, bank account draining, and inevitable PTSD associated with the randomness and excruciating slow pace of litigation. Although they mean well, insurance agents are no substitute for a business attorney who understands litigation from the trenches.

Seventy-five percent of businesses in the United States are underinsured by 40% or more.[5] When it comes to insurance, our advice to our clients is to have a good business lawyer review their insurance policy. Your business lawyer should know most aspects of your business and its associated risks and have read the exclusions in your policy to advise you on either avoiding those activities or buying riders to include them.

Do not risk spending money on insurance that will not be there when you need it most. We've seen this happen too many times.

> DO NOT RISK SPENDING MONEY ON INSURANCE THAT WILL NOT BE THERE WHEN YOU NEED IT MOST.

A few years ago, an online travel agency hired us to perform a CM6. The company's young, cost-conscious owners had purchased a general liability policy with low limits, high deductibles, and minimal cybersecurity coverage. During the audit, we advised them to max out their cyber coverage because they were an e-commerce company and were still very young with minimal compliance mechanisms in place. Thankfully, they took our advice.

Within 90 days, almost like clockwork, a "hacktivist" group attacked them with a massive data breach, exposing many of their clients' credit card information on the dark web. Because we reviewed their policy as part of their CM6, spotted their weaknesses, and advised them to fill the gap, and because they took our advice, they didn't have to shutter their doors. Their policy kicked in and paid the hundreds of thousands of dollars needed for security costs, former FBI negotiators, forensic audits, legal fees from the top (and most expensive) firms in the country, as well as damages, to work with the hackers and remediate the breach.

Without our legal review, they would have been woefully underinsured and faced government regulators on their dime. Thanks to the timely increase in policy coverage, our client was saved from financial ruin, and operations continued with minimal interruption. Today, our client is a growing, thriving business instead of a bankruptcy debtor.

Not All Policies Are Created Equal

Another reason lawyers need to review insurance policies is that many agencies and carriers offer cookie-cutter, one-size-fits-all policies based on a company's industry.

Things get more complicated when the business operates in different industries. For example, an independent car dealer may *also* have a related finance company, a real estate business, and a warranty company. An insurance agent may need more carrier support and policy specificity. A good business lawyer who understands the client's operations, revenue streams, and future vision can use a scalpel instead of a sledgehammer to get the client the specific coverage he needs.

Furthermore, highly regulated companies require specialized insurance. Companies with many employees should consider Employment Practices Liability Insurance (EPLI) to cover employee claims. Companies involved in mergers and acquisitions should consider coverage for claims related to the deal (like representations and warranties coverage or directors and officers liability coverage) and tail coverage for, among other things, claims that pre-date the deal. An M&A (mergers and acquisitions) lawyer is more suitable than a non-specialized insurance agent in these cases. If any of the above situations apply to you, have you had those discussions with your insurance agent?

We are in the business of protecting your business, and we do not consider ourselves successful if we are only putting out fires—success is avoiding the fires altogether. We look at the sparks and attack them before they smolder, before the six horsemen knock on your door to fan the flames. If you are ready to begin this proactive approach, let's start building your six-sided fortress.

Chapter 1: Customers

CUSTOMERS ARE THE LIFEBLOOD of any enterprise and represent both loyal patrons and potential litigants. For both product and service-based businesses, the moment a customer starts interacting with your business, even if he doesn't buy a thing from you, he is a potential plaintiff.

In this chapter, we detail the three point-of-sale scenarios: written customer contracts, face-to-face transactions, and online customers.

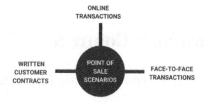

Top Takeaways From Chapter 1:

- You must write a well-crafted customer contract tailored to your industry and your company's specific needs.

- Disclaimers, limitations of liability, election of remedies, forum selection, attorney fees provisions, and dispute resolution provisions are vital elements in that contract.'

- The CM6 five-step "waterfall dispute resolution clause" is the low-hanging fruit of all contracts, is extremely effective at keeping you out of court, and is grossly overlooked. You should include it in almost EVERY contract you sign.

- Indemnification clauses can shift liability away from the business owner to the customer for the use of the product.

- To avoid premises liability, storefront owners should post notices and take reasonable precautions to eliminate or mitigate any condition or circumstance that could injure another person.

- Websites must comply with certain norms, standards, obligations, and laws, including the Americans with Disabilities Act (ADA).

Review all the bulleted suggestions throughout this chapter, as well as those in Appendix B of this book, for additional considerations for your customer agreements. (See p. 133)

Written Customer Contracts

Tailored contracts serve three main functions:

1. They protect your liability and risk.

2. They protect your bottom line.

3. They create certainty, clarity, and specificity to a greater extent than not having good ones.

The contract is the first document a plaintiff's lawyer reviews when she decides whether to bring suit. Our team becomes intentionally paranoid and protective when we draft contracts. We spend hours picking apart the contract, trying to find ambiguities and inconsistencies, and squeezing in exceptions wherever we can.

The reality is that after the purchase, the next time anyone usually looks at the contract is when they want to sue you, but before the transaction, they probably don't even bother to read it. To protect our client, we draft the customer contract (or order form or "terms and conditions," depending on the type of transaction it is) to make it as "pro-client" as we can. We make this wall of the fort as high and as strong as a court or arbitrator will enforce. You can always back off from a provision that's too harsh, but it's really hard to make it more protective later, after the fact.

You can present the contract to your customer in multiple ways. You can go old school with paper and ink, or you can use a click-through signature on a secure, reputable app like DocuSign®. We recommend electronic signatures—less paper to get lost or damaged and more evidence of an agreement.

A well-crafted customer contract is vital whether selling products or providing services. It should clearly outline the agreement's material terms and conditions. Significant problems come from the following pain points:

- Detail concerning contract scope

- Mechanisms for amendment

- The parties' intent

- Remedies for non-performance

- Lack of specificity in other terms

- Inappropriate contract structure

- Disputes over pricing

- Identification of parties required for liability or performance, including affiliates and subcontractors

Your contract is the first line of defense, so protect yourself as a business owner. The customer may always be right, but the business owner should always be in control. When writing customer contracts, the rule of thumb is to protect yourself as a business owner.

> THE CUSTOMER MAY ALWAYS BE RIGHT, BUT THE BUSINESS OWNER SHOULD ALWAYS BE IN CONTROL.

Here are essential considerations in drafting an airtight customer contract:

- The contract should address each of the points above.

- It should protect the business, its owners, and its employees to the fullest extent.

- It must address specific industry scenarios.

- It should be specific to your customers and products.

Realistically, you should have a seasoned business lawyer draft your agreements (all of them, not just your customer contracts). Pick a lawyer who has drafted hundreds, if not thousands, of commercial agreements to draft yours. Ask them to send you the templates and checklists they used to draft your contract. If they refuse because their egos will be bruised, find another lawyer. If they aren't using good, lengthy, clean templates and checklists, they're being lazy. And if they're just copying and pasting from a contract they used for another client, they're not just being lazy; they're being stupid. That's a recipe for leaving something in that they should have taken out or taking out something they should have left in.

Disclaimers, Limitations of Liability, and Remedies

Every contract should have a disclaimer that states the products and services being sold are being purchased by the customer "as is" and with "no warranty whatsoever to the fullest extent permitted by law." There should also be a provision concerning a limitation of liability. This is where the customer is limited in how much he can pursue from the business in damages. The liability should be limited to the amount of the purchase itself or some other nominal amount, like $500. This is also where the customer waives the ability to sue for punitive damages or to assert a claim as part of a class action.

Disclaimers of all warranties in contracts must be conspicuous. Customers frequently sign contracts without reading them, and courts disfavor boilerplate language where bargaining power is greatly disparate. Increasing the visibility of disclaimers on the page of a contract (by using increased font sizes and/or boldface font and event segmenting this language into separate paragraphs or pages) can improve your chances of enforceability in court if you end up in one. Many states, like Ohio, require the conspicuousness of disclaimer and/or limitation of liability language for enforceability, so give them good headings, make them ALL CAPS, and separate them from the rest of the contract.

Anytime you take someone's rights away, the court scrutinizes that provision closely. An experienced lawyer must carefully draft disclaimers, waivers, forum selection clauses, and attorney fee transfers. Drafting this is not a DIY situation. If you get it wrong, the court will strike the provision. Or worse, you may be violating a consumer protection law by having unconscionable provisions in your contracts.

Liability should also be limited to the customer's specific use of the product according to its specifications. There should be no liability for the customer's illegal use or any other misuse of the product or services or for their use by anyone other than the customer.

To sum up, your contract should contain at least the following provisions:

- Detailed *and* general disclaimers of all warranties in a separate paragraph, written in highly conspicuous font size and lettering.

- Caps on the amounts that customers can recover from the business (for example, capping claims at the purchase amount or a nominal amount like $500).

- A waiver of the customer's ability to sue in a class action.

- Limitations on the customer's ability to recover non-compensatory damages, such as speculative, punitive, or trebled.

- A section stating the only remedy for customers is a return or refund.

- An assurance that no other compensation is available beyond the remedy already provided.

- A requirement that the customer properly use the product or service according to the law and instructions provided.

- A statement that there is no liability for use by third parties.

Jurisdiction, Forum Selection, and Choice of Law

- Jurisdiction: a court's ability to reach and affect you

- Forum Selection: the venue or location where your dispute will be heard

- Choice of law: the state law that will be applied to the facts of the case at the time of court or arbitral resolution

When drafting and negotiating your contracts, be sure to have the customer submit to the jurisdiction of your home state's courts (including to enforce an arbitration award). Ensure also that they agree that the venue for disputes should be in the state and federal courts situated in your county. If you do end up in court, you want it to be in your backyard, not the customer's. This will save you a ton of money in legal fees, transportation costs, other logistics headaches, and wasted time. Home court advantage is a huge point of leverage in a lawsuit avoidance or lawsuit settlement strategy.

Assuming you choose arbitration as your ultimate dispute resolution forum, specify that an arbitration hearing must take place in your county. Regarding which state law governs, you may choose either your home state or a neutral and business-friendly state like New York or Delaware. You should discuss with counsel which state is optimal.

Attorney Fees

The attorneys' fees clause ensures that if you must sue to recover funds owed to you, the customer will be responsible for paying your attorneys' fees and all other costs associated with the lawsuit. Remember that the price of a business attorney to handle a contract dispute can range from thousands to hundreds of thousands of dollars. Therefore, it is essential to include this provision when drafting your contract.

On the other hand, if you have to defend a lawsuit (or a counterclaim) and lose, a *mutual* attorney fee provision may require you to pay the other side's costs. In some jurisdictions, good drafting can make attorneys' fees available for collections suits, with each party paying its own fees for non-collections suits.

Court Scrutiny

A business attorney must carefully draft the above disclaimers, waivers, clauses, and provisions because courts closely scrutinize provisions that take away someone's rights, especially his right to a day in court. A seasoned business lawyer can help you avoid the risk of having the provisions struck down or, worse, violating consumer protection laws with unconscionable contract terms and the court ordering heavy fines.

Warning: Different Industries Have Different Standards

Different industries have varying regulations concerning the contract's acceptable and enforceable terms and conditions. Therefore, it is crucial to have a lawyer familiar with your company's industry and regulations review your agreement. State-specific laws may forbid clauses or demand specific language. Your lawyer should:

- Create well-drafted provisions that comply with industry-specific regulations.

- Ensure that contract language is clear and concise and accurately reflects the parties' intentions.

- Research current guidelines concerning the enforceability of specific terms relative to specific types of parties (e.g., business customers versus individual consumers).

Waterfall Dispute Resolution Provisions

The low-hanging fruit of courtroom avoidance is the five-step waterfall dispute resolution provision. We are absolutely dumbfounded when lawyers don't put them into their clients' agreements. We add them to all our contracts (not just the customer ones) to prevent needless litigation. This provision establishes a framework for addressing customer disputes by defining a process for customers to notify the company of any issues and allowing the company to address them before formal litigation.

The five-step process works like this:

1. The customer submits a written notice of the dispute.

2. The company has thirty days to address the issue(s).

3. Senior executives of both entities meet if the dispute persists.

4. If the issue still isn't resolved, the parties attend a non-binding mediation, with costs shared equally.

5. If the problem remains unresolved, the parties attend a binding, confidential, expedited arbitration within six months of the original dispute.

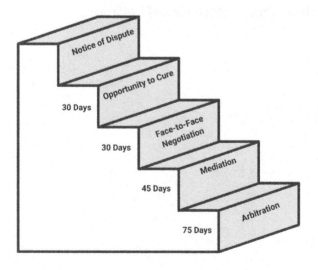

You can play around with the above timelines but don't mess with the five steps.

Courts take seriously their responsibility to give everyone their day in court. Companies must, therefore, take extra steps to ensure their provisions are reasonable and not buried in boilerplate language.

To maximize enforceability, the waterfall dispute provision should be:

- Well-drafted in specific and understandable language

- Conspicuous

- Enforceable in your particular industry

- Drafted as a separate provision/distinct paragraph (ideally on its own page)

- Have a separate customer signature or initial

The waterfall dispute provision saves time and money because, if drafted correctly, a court will likely kick a case out of the courtroom upon the company's filing of a motion to stay to compel arbitration or dispute resolution. Courts love clearing their dockets. Let's make it easy for them when someone tries to sue *you*.

Indemnification Clauses

Indemnification clauses shift responsibility away from the business or its owners and onto the customer if any claims arise from the customer's use or misuse of a product or service.

Indemnification clauses enable a contracting party to adjust the level of risk it is willing to accept for each transaction and each counterparty. They provide protection from damages and lawsuits that the counterparty can more efficiently bear.

An effective indemnification provision benefits both the indemnified and the indemnifying party. The indemnified party can recover attorneys' fees and other expenses, which are usually not recoverable otherwise unless a statute allows it (which is rare).

Components of a typical indemnification clause include:

- **Obligation to indemnify:** The indemnifying party must reimburse the indemnified party for paid costs and expenses and make advance payment for unpaid costs and expenses such as liabilities, claims, and causes of action.

- **Obligation to defend:** The indemnifying party must either provide counsel at its expense or reimburse or make advance payment for *defense* costs and expenses. The indemnifying party may require the right to assume and control the defense of the third-party suit, which is okay so long as you can participate in the defense at your own cost (you may want your own advisor involved and overseeing the matter).

- **"Hold harmless" provisions:** The indemnifying party releases the indemnified party from any responsibility for damage or other liability caused by the indemnifying party. The release shifts the legal risk for any damage or liability caused by the indemnifying party to the indemnifying party by cutting off the indemnified party from responsibility for the harm done.

A Note about Arbitration

Arbitration is a dispute resolution process different from mediation, in which a neutral third party (an arbitrator) hears arguments from both sides and makes a binding decision. It is an alternative to traditional court litigation where the parties agree to abide by the arbitrator's decision, which is typically final and not subject to appeal, except in limited circumstances.

There are at least two philosophies on the arbitration process. Some lawyers think arbitration makes good cases into bad cases and prefer litigation in a traditional courtroom setting. Other lawyers (like us) prefer arbitration, where the decision is confidential, and clients have more control over the selection of the decision maker. For example, in court, the decision-makers include elected judges who may know nothing about your industry and random jurors who know even less.

Speak with your attorney about what her approach is to your matter.

Overall, the goal is to keep your company out of the courtroom and keep your money in your pocket rather than your lawyers' pocket.

We, therefore, put dispute resolution clauses into every contract we draft for our clients, including employment agreements, confidentiality agreements, stock purchase agreements, shareholder agreements, and landlord-tenant disputes.

> THE GOAL IS TO KEEP YOUR COMPANY OUT OF THE COURTROOM AND KEEP YOUR MONEY IN YOUR POCKET RATHER THAN YOUR LAWYERS' POCKET.

Face-to-Face Transactions

Premises Liability

Property owners have a duty to maintain their property in a safe condition and to warn visitors of any known hazards. If a property owner fails to meet this duty and a visitor is injured, the property owner may be held liable for the injuries and damages sustained by the visitor.

Premises liability is one of the most significant sources of exposure for storefront owners.[6] There are a few things to keep in mind:

- You owe your customers a duty of care to ensure that there are no hazardous circumstances, objects, or materials that could cause harm on the premises, no matter what they are coming to buy (or even if they don't buy anything at all).

- The standards of care that apply to people on your premises vary based on their reason for being there. "Invited" customers (who don't really require an invitation—they're invited if they are there to do business) have higher protections than those on the premises for their purposes or who are trespassing.[7]

- The most effective way to address premises liability, regardless of why someone is on your property, is to ensure that the premises do not expose anyone entering to any foreseeable harm. Owners must take reasonable precautions to eliminate or mitigate any condition or circumstance that could injure another person.

- If it's not possible to remove a hazard, the owner should have clearly visible notices warning the customer of the danger and should take all reasonable steps to protect them through remediation and guardrail-type efforts.

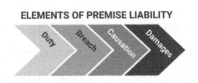

ELEMENTS OF PREMISE LIABILITY

Additional information on reducing the risk of premises liability claims is available in Appendix C (see p. 151).

Contracts from Signs or Notices

While maxing out your insurance to cover premises liability is a big part of your protection, signage, notices, receipts, and order confirmations create contracts. For instance, airlines provide passengers with a baggage tag that includes terms and conditions that they agree to. Similarly, signs or agreements in your store can clarify that customers purchase items at their own risk, helping establish that they assume responsibility for their safety while on your property and limiting your liability in the event of accidents or injuries. These provisions protect both your customers and your business. They are not foolproof, but they can definitely form the basis of liability limitation.

Reducing Premise Liability Risks

We recommend following this step-by-step process to identify, evaluate, and remedy premises liability risks.

1. Understand what premises liability is. (Great news! By reading this book, you just got a little closer.)

2. Conduct a risk assessment for your premises.

3. Manage risks through corrective action.

4. Provide adequate security for your premises. In addition to slip-and-fall incidents, insufficient security measures can result in premises liability claims. Businesses can be held responsible for customer robberies or attacks that occur on their property due to inadequate security.

5. Periodically spot-check for hazards and immediately take responsive action.

6. Use signage to warn customers of hazards while fixing them.

By ensuring customer safety and using contracts to your advantage, you can reduce the risk of liability and ensure the long-term success of your business.

Online Customers

Though this chapter is dedicated to plaintiff customers, when discussing online customers, the below sections are government-driven and could have just as easily gone into our Government chapter. We've added it here because they should be part of any business's customer compliance checklist.

Website Compliance

The first online customer consideration is your website, which must comply with certain norms, standards, and obligations. In a sense, your website is a contract with your customers and may create obligations you must adhere to.

Americans with Disabilities Act

One of these obligations is with the Americans with Disabilities Act (ADA). The US Department of Justice has consistently maintained that public accommodations, including internet offerings, must comply with the ADA in all aspects of goods, services, and activities. In addition, you must design your website to be accessible to people with disabilities. It must include accessibility features and design elements that accommodate people with all abilities that may otherwise have impaired access to your website. These abilities and their accommodations include but are not limited to:

- Auditory

- Cognitive

- Neurological

- Physical

- Speech

- Visual

We highly recommend using a third-party accessibility checker to audit your website for ADA compliance and conducting a self-audit with your website developer using an ADA website compliance checklist.

A website accessibility checklist is available in Appendix M. (See p. 225)

Consumer Protection Laws

Next, you must consider state and federal consumer protection laws for online customers. Regulatory bodies, such as state attorneys general and the Federal Trade Commission (FTC), enforce these laws.

Not only should you ensure your business operations, including the content and claims of your website, do not violate these laws, but you must not attempt to waive responsibilities that the law cannot waive. Your business lawyer's up-to-date legal research into your industry-specific rules and regulations will identify these for you.

Consumer protection law violation comes with a big price tag. The FTC has a range of enforcement tools, including the "Notice of Penalty Offenses." This document lists certain unfair or deceptive conduct that violates the FTC Act.[8] If your business engages in any conduct covered in the notice, you risk facing civil penalties of up to $46,517 per violation. Ouch!

You must understand the consumer protection laws that apply to your business and work with your business attorney to organize a compliance program to avoid violations.

Data Protection and Privacy

Protecting data and privacy is a crucial liability consideration for your website and commercial operations. To ensure protection, we advise having online terms and conditions and a privacy policy on your site. A cyber law attorney should draft these documents with regulatory compliance and data protection in mind.

Every situation is different, but adopting policies and procedures, such as an Information Security Policy, can reduce the likelihood of unauthorized access to business and consumer information. If you have trade secrets or have entered confidentiality agreements, you may need to take extra steps to protect confidential information.

It is also essential to have an internal cyber incident response plan to handle data breaches and ensure compliance with data breach laws. These policies and cyber insurance coverage can potentially save your business.

⋙ ⋘

Businesses must protect themselves from litigation risks coming from customers. Working with a business lawyer to ensure compliance with laws and draft proper contracts and policies is imperative. For more information on clauses in customer contracts, see Appendix B (on p. 133).

In the next chapter, we will explore the legal considerations involved in vendor relationships to minimize risks and maximize opportunities.

Chapter 2: Vendors

V ENDOR CONTRACTS ARE KEY to most businesses. But how do you protect your business from the unexpected? From negotiating terms and conditions to managing disputes, we cover everything you need to know in this chapter to ensure a successful partnership with your vendors.

Top Takeaways From Chapter 2:

- When dealing with vendors, apply a customer-centric approach by ensuring you protect your business and negotiate the contract's terms and conditions.

- To minimize risk, have your lawyer review vendor contracts with you to ensure they meet your business needs.

- Draft your own terms and conditions to protect your business and avoid contract disputes.

- Your terms and conditions document should include explicit warranties, provisions for the right to inspect goods, and the ability to maximize the remedies available for non-conforming goods.

- Use indemnification provisions to shift liability away from your company.

Consider Jane, a business owner who placed a large order with a vendor. Excited about the potential profits this new product would generate for her business, she eagerly awaited delivery. When the products arrived, though, she quickly realized that something was seriously wrong. The items were faulty and unusable, leaving her with a warehouse full of useless merchandise and a sinking feeling in her gut.

Immediately, Jane contacted the vendor to report the issue and request a refund, but he refused to take responsibility for the faulty products. As a result, she was left with a significant financial loss, lots of egg on her face, and no clear path forward.

This is a nightmare scenario for any business owner. Unfortunately, it is not uncommon. Vendor contracts are crucial to running a successful business when properly drafted, but they can be a minefield of potential pitfalls and risks when they're not.

Empowering Your Business: The Customer-Centric Approach to Vendor Contracts

When dealing with vendors, remember *you* are the customer. Take everything we talked about in the last chapter, but reverse it.

Apply the same protective measures to your vendor contracts so you receive the same protection that your customers want with you. To approach these

> IN VENDOR CONTRACTS, REMEMBER YOU ARE THE CUSTOMER.

contracts with a customer-centric approach, keep the following in mind:

- Do not assume the contract from your vendor protects you; protecting yourself is your responsibility.

- All provisions in Chapter 1, including the waterfall dispute resolution provision, are essential in vendor contracts but reversed, affording yourself maximum protection.

- Include clear warranties and remedies for breach and remove disclaimers and limitations that will leave you empty-handed when you do not get what you expect.

- Review the contract closely and ensure specificity regarding time, place, manner, and scope of work/delivery.

- Leverage plays a big role.

When I draft a contract for my client when they are the customer, I want lots of warranties without limitations and no disclaimers. I want neutral jurisdiction, venue, and choice of law provisions, too. I don't want them hauled into a courtroom in their vendor's backyard if it's inconvenient for their company.

Leverage

Leverage plays a big role. Vendors may present one-sided contracts with disclaimers, liability limitations, and other language that make it difficult for you to seek relief in the event of a dispute. Do not assume you must accept such language. Consider the leverage you have in the vendor contract negotiation process. There may be limited room for negotiation when dealing with large companies like Microsoft® or Amazon. But when dealing with smaller vendors, you may have more bargaining power than you think you do.

Begin by identifying the contracts that impact your business most and have your lawyer review them with you. One way to do that is by looking at your profit and loss statements. See where your biggest expenses are. Generally, you're paying the most for the inputs in your business that you need the most. Pick three to five vendors that are the most critical to your business. Even if it's just one contract, it's better than just signing whatever the supplier puts in front of you.

Work carefully through the deliverables. Make sure they are specific in time, place, manner, and scope of work. Be as specific as possible. Your vendor is going to give you a one-sided contract drafted by their lawyer in the same way that you are doing with your customer contract. They will be disclaiming warranties, limiting liability and remedies, and making it as difficult as possible for you to get any relief if you have a dispute. Do not assume that you have to accept that language.

When reviewing vendor contracts with your lawyer, ask him to:

- Spell out the warranties you expect.

- Identify the remedies available if the vendor breaches those warranties.

- Include a five-step waterfall dispute resolution provision.

- Choose a neutral place to resolve disputes.

- Ensure any language regarding attorney fees is mutual.

- Consider including a confidentiality and non-disparagement provision in the contract.

Our clients sometimes push back when we suggest changes to their vendor contracts. They worry that sending the contract to the legal department will delay closing the deal or, worse, kill it entirely. We usually address these concerns through negotiation or a phone call.

Assess the non-negotiable terms in the contract and draft them carefully to minimize your business's exposure. Also, focus on the 20% of the changes that will address 80% of the risk rather than asking for everything.

Standard Terms and Conditions

One important way to protect yourself when entering vendor contracts is by drafting your own terms and conditions. You need your own set if you spend a lot of money with numerous or particular vendors. Seventy-seven percent of companies experience one or more contract disputes yearly, with 43% related to contract terms and conditions.[9] You can avoid these by submitting your own terms and having the vendor either agree or comment.

Your terms and conditions document is a general document you provide to your vendors, just like you would provide a general customer agreement to your customers. Do not rely on the standard terms and conditions in ancillary documents like emails, quotes, or invoices to avoid contract disputes.

Your terms and conditions should:

- Be attached or linked to, and expressly incorporated into, every generated purchase order.

- Explicitly reject the other party's terms and require an agreement to *your* terms as a condition of the contract.

- Include vendor warranties that state the goods comply with the specifications provided, definitive shipping dates, and a requirement for sufficiently protective packaging that complies with applicable regulations.

- Provide the right to inspect the goods before acceptance.

- Provide the right to accept or reject all or a portion of the goods.

- Provide the ability to maximize the remedies available for non-conforming goods.

- Require a full warranty that the purchased items or services will be merchantable and fit for the purpose communicated to the vendor.

- Include a five-step waterfall dispute resolution provision, remedies available for breach of warranties, a forum selection clause in a neutral jurisdiction, and a statement that you will be entitled to all remedies available at law.

Depending on the circumstances of the deal and who has the relative leverage, the vendor may agree to sell goods and services according to your terms and conditions. If not, ask them to identify the objectionable terms. If they refuse to agree to any of your terms and conditions, make a business decision, fully informed of the risks, whether to proceed with the transaction.

Indemnifications

Recall from Chapter 1 that indemnification can shift liability away from your company. In a customer contract, you want your customer to indemnify, defend, and pay your legal fees if you get sued for his use or misuse of your product or service. But in vendor contracts, seek indemnification from your vendor if you use or resell its product and it causes damage to you or anyone else.

There are two types of indemnification: first-party and third-party. First-party indemnification applies when the vendor's products or services directly harm you. Third-party indemnification applies when the vendor's product or services injure a third party and sues you for it. The objective is to transfer liability to the supplier because it has complete control over the product's design, manufacturing, and distribution.

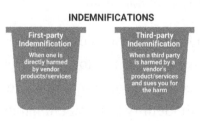

INDEMNIFICATIONS

First-party Indemnification
When one is directly harmed by vendor products/services

Third-party Indemnification
When a third party is harmed by a vendor's product/services and sues you for the harm

Services Agreement

You should have a reliable services agreement if you work with consultants or independent contractors. A service agreement should:

- List the details about the provided services, including completion dates and what standards you will use to evaluate their sufficiency;

- Include warranties that the services will be provided in a suitable, professional, and workman-like manner, consistent with industry standards;

- *Not* include any disclaimers or limitations on liability or damages;

- Include a provision that payment for the services should be conditioned on your determination that the services are sufficient, and if you find them to be subpar, you should have the ability to dispute the charges and get a refund;

- Include a provision that a contractor is required to get your prior written approval before incurring any expenses and is solely responsible for any expenses incurred without your consent

- Include a provision that requires the contractor to assign all intellectual property rights to you.

Again, review the other bulleted suggestions throughout this chapter and Appendix F (p. 173) in this book for additional considerations for your vendor agreements.

Purchasing Policy

Standardization helps inexperienced employees who may require guidance when handling procurement contracts. A purchasing policy should be created for key personnel or the entire company, requiring the employee to send the standard purchase terms and conditions to the vendor prior to consummating a purchase.

The purchasing policy should require enhanced caution or management approval of a material contract triggered by a particular escalation event. For example, the policy may be triggered by purchases exceeding a certain amount, such as $1,000 or $5,000, or by the type of purchase being made, including the length of the contract and exposure term.

The Playbook

After your legal counsel has reviewed and negotiated your top three to five vendor agreements and you have implemented a standard purchasing policy, some vendors may still request changes to terms and conditions. Vendor requests typically follow common patterns. They may, for example, include requests to change jurisdiction or attorney fee-shifting provisions. In essence, they want your contract to be a little bit more reasonable towards them.

Rather than involving your lawyer each time, create a playbook with pre-approved responses for routine changes. Include language protecting your

CREATE A PLAYBOOK WITH PRE-APPROVED RESPONSES FOR ROUTINE CHANGES.

employees from accusations of unlicensed practice of law.[10]

The playbook may take the form of a table where the left-hand column has the type of change requested, and the right-hand column either permits, rejects, or offers alternative language for the change. This is an excellent tool but requires training and a semi-sophisticated businessperson who understands basic contract principles and drafting considerations to make the changes.

The more contracts and changes are signed, transmitted, and redlined over time, the more intelligent the playbook will be—it is a living and flexible document. If you are an in-house lawyer, having a playbook for your purchasers and other management-level team members will save you and your staff a lot of time responding to their contract-related requests.

The best way to protect your business is to apply the same level of protection to your company in both customer and vendor contracts. By reviewing and negotiating contracts, you can avoid costly legal battles and maintain strong business relationships.

Remember, you are the customer in these contracts and should want the same things in the vendor agreement that your customer wants in their agreement with you. You want to limit your liability and ensure your remedies are there, shifting the risk of the other party's acts or omissions to them.

Please reference Appendix F: Must-Have Clauses in Vendor Contracts on page 173 for additional resources.

The next chapter will discuss important legal considerations for business owners, shareholders, and partners. Addressing these issues can further protect your business and ensure its success.

Chapter 3: Owners, Shareholders, and Partners

S TARTING A BUSINESS IS thrilling. Safeguarding personal assets as a business owner is vital.

The state and federal governments in the United States have made a pretty sweet deal with business owners: You take risks and do it without committing fraud and checking a few boxes, and we will protect your personal assets from liability. You help the government turn the wheels of commerce, and it will help you take smart risks. This deal encourages job creation, tax revenue, putting food on the table, sending your kids to college, and generating employee benefits. Everybody wins, so long as you follow the rules.

This chapter discusses important considerations for business owners, shareholders, and partners, including selecting a state to incorporate, appointing a statutory agent, indicating the time of business formation, drafting governance documents, estate planning, and piercing the corporate veil.

Top Takeaways From Chapter 3:

- Incorporation is necessary for business owners to protect their personal assets.

- When incorporating, it's important to consider factors like anonymity, confidentiality, tax treatment, and stakeholder rights and obligations and to involve an attorney and certified public accountant in the process.

- New entities are not properly formed until all necessary steps have been taken, including obtaining an EIN, adopting governance documents, and opening a separate bank account. Filing with the Secretary of State is not the sole indicator of formation.

- Governance documents, such as bylaws and operating agreements, vary by entity and are necessary to preserve limited liability protection.

- Owners, shareholders, and partners can avoid probate, provide a detailed distribution of assets, and create another level of limited liability protection with expertly crafted estate plans.

- Limited liability companies are not bulletproof when it comes to protecting owners' personal assets. A plaintiff may be able to pierce the corporate veil and access personal assets in certain circumstances.

Crucial Considerations When Beginning Your Business

Incorporation

Once you have decided to start your business, you must file a certificate of formation (or whatever your state calls it) with the state's Secretary of State as a corporation, limited liability corporation (LLC), limited partnership, or another limited liability entity. It doesn't necessarily have to be your state, of course. Some states like Delaware, Nevada, New York, and Ohio allow you to incorporate without identifying the owners, giving them added anonymity. Many business owners file in non-home states based on this and other considerations like favorable tax treatment and lack of annual fees and filings, among others.

Involve your attorney and CPA in the analysis to determine the best state and tax elections. With your accountant, identify all states where your business has a tax nexus and understand its requirements for sales tax, payroll tax, commercial activity tax, and other taxes. You will register with the Department of Revenue in that state because you are now transacting business there, and it will want its cut.

By default, corporations are taxed as "C corporations" for tax purposes, whereas LLCs are taxed as partnerships or disregarded entities based on the number of owners. Whether you choose an LLC or corporation for your business, electing "S corporation" tax status may be beneficial. This election makes the company a "pass-through entity," meaning that its income counts as personal income, and you avoid double taxation associated with C-corporation status. Additionally, S corporations can pay salaries to owners and avoid self-employment tax on non-salary profits, providing a potential tax advantage depending on your circumstances. S Corporations are not possible in certain circumstances, for example, where shareholders are not natural persons (with some exceptions like Q-sub trusts), exceed one hundred in number, or are non-resident aliens.

A choice of entity type flowchart is available in Appendix H (see p. 201).

Statutory Agent

The second step when creating your business is making sure that you have a Statutory Agent identified in your Secretary of State filings. When filing formation documents with the Secretary of State for the state where you decide to form your business, your filing must comply with the state's formation requirements. Every state requires the appointment of a registered agent, sometimes referred to as a statutory agent. The statutory agent receives service of process, lawsuit notices, and tax notices, among others.

Business owners should choose a lawyer or a third-party company as their statutory agent to maintain anonymity. This provides anonymity and more certainty that the notices will be received, even after you've moved homes or offices. Most states require a physical address, but some allow a P.O. Box or other virtual location.

Time of Business Formation

Contrary to popular belief, new entities are not simply formed when the Secretary of State issues a certificate. You must complete these four steps to properly form a business.

STEPS FOR BUSINESS FORMATION

1 FORMATION PAPERWORK

2 ACQUIRE EIN

3 GOVERNING DOCUMENTS

4 CORPORATE BANK ACCOUNT

Don't forget to complete all four steps.

Governance Documents

To preserve limited liability protection, adopt well-drafted governance documents and formation paperwork filed with the Secretary of State. These documents vary by type of entity but generally include the following distinctions:

- The owners of a corporation are called shareholders, and they typically need Bylaws and a Shareholders' Agreement to govern meetings,

voting, directors, officers, and shareholder relationships. Corporations must annually elect or appoint a board of directors.

- Close corporations simplify governance under one
  document by abolishing the board of directors,
  thereby eliminating the need for Bylaws (also called
  a Code of Regulations).

- Owners of an LLC are called members, and they
  use an Operating Agreement to govern corpo-
  rate-level decision-making.

- Limited and general partnerships have partners
  and use partnership agreements.

- Close corporations and LLCs must adopt written resolutions for significant or outside-the-ordi-
  nary-course-of-business decisions, as well as periodic or year-end resolutions.

- All decisions must comply with the entity's governance and formation documents and applicable
  business laws.

The agreements should anticipate future growth, tax,
and accounting concerns. Also, as with all agreements
described throughout this book, they should include a
five-step waterfall dispute resolution provision.

A seasoned business lawyer, experienced in drafting complex shareholder agreements, should draft these documents. Avoid inexperienced lawyers and online services that will draft governance documents that may not apply to your company or the owners' specific needs, interests, and circumstances.

> A SEASONED BUSINESS LAWYER, EXPERIENCED IN DRAFTING COMPLEX SHAREHOLDER AGREEMENTS, SHOULD DRAFT THESE DOCUMENTS.

Estate Planning

If you own a business, you should hold your interests in your company inside of a trust.

Most company owners hold their interests directly, meaning they are the direct holders of their shares in the company. However, savvy and experienced business lawyers recommend that shareholders have estate plans drafted by an expert estate planning lawyer knowledgeable in tax law, who can help avoid probate by drafting solid trust documents for their clients. They can also state in the trust document a highly detailed distribution of assets to heirs and create another level of limited liability between the owner's assets and the company's risks and liabilities. While the LLC acts as a shield between the owner's assets and the company's liabilities, a trust acts as a second shield. We therefore highly recommend adding an estate planning attorney to the legal team.

Piercing the Corporate Veil

It is vital to protect your personal assets through LLCs and corporations, which offer limited liability protection and shield you from personal responsibility for your business's debts. But this protection is not foolproof. A plaintiff can sue and "pierce the corporate veil," meaning they can go beyond your entity protection and get to your personal assets. Though it is not easy, a plaintiff can pierce the veil if they prove any of the following:

- The corporate entity is just a front for the owners, an "alter ego."

- The owner used the corporation to commit fraud or other illegal acts.

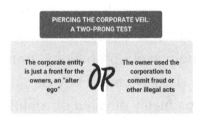

The plaintiff must also demonstrate that they suffered harm or loss due to the owner's wrongdoing.

Prong One: Alter Ego

This doctrine applies to owners who treat their business as their own personal entity, blurring the lines between personal and professional. An LLC or corporation should be treated as a separate legal entity, but if an owner fails to maintain the corporate entity's separate legal status, he leaves himself vulnerable to arguments for piercing the veil.

Owners can prevent piercing the veil through alter ego theory through the following:

- Avoid commingling, mixing personal accounts/funds with company accounts/funds.

- Implement systems to prevent commingling.

- Avoid using company property for personal use.

- Ensure company assets and liabilities are fully contained within the company.

- Document the use of all company expenses and reimbursements, especially those that could appear personal.

- Use corporate credit cards rather than personal ones for company purchases.

- Ensure adequate capitalization of your company: avoid giving yourself distributions or dividends that could leave the company without enough capital to pay its obligations.

Regarding undercapitalization, the amount of money that constitutes adequate capitalization varies depending on your business and industry. If a distribution or dividend leaves your company unable to pay its debts, your creditors may be able to pierce the veil and come after your personal assets. Consulting with an experienced business attorney will help determine the appropriate amount of capitalization for your company and avoid risky practices that could put your assets at risk.

Prong Two: Fraud and Illegality

In general, fraud and illegality arise when an owner intentionally uses a corporation or LLC to commit a dishonest or illegal act that harms another person or entity. The owner cannot hide behind limited liability protection in these circumstances.

Fraud is defined differently from state to state, but here is what generally constitutes the core of fraud:

- The owner or company makes a representation (or conceals information while under the duty to disclose).

- The representation or omission is material to a transaction.

- The representation was false, and the owner knew it at the time.

- The owner or company intended to mislead the other person into relying on the misrepresentation.

- The other person justifiably relied on the owner's misrepresentation.

- Injury to the other person resulted from the misrepresentation.

If there is any suspicion that certain representations or activity may be fraudulent or criminal, you should discuss it with your attorney and inquire whether there are alternative methods that accomplish your goal.

Additionally, incurring debt while insolvent or knowingly purchasing goods or services that a corporation cannot afford to pay for is a basis for piercing the corporate veil. It is important for corporations to maintain proper financial records and manage their debts responsibly to avoid exposing their shareholders to personal liability.

Proper legal structuring and compliance with corporate formalities are essential for businesses to maintain legal protection and mitigate litigation risks. However, companies may still face legal challenges from the government, such as compliance lawsuits and investigations. The next chapter will discuss how the government may sue a business, the different types of government enforcement actions, and how companies can prepare for and respond to such actions.

> PROPER LEGAL STRUCTURING AND COMPLIANCE WITH CORPORATE FORMALITIES ARE ESSENTIAL FOR BUSINESSES TO MAINTAIN LEGAL PROTECTION AND MITIGATE LITIGATION RISKS.

Chapter 4: Government

Whether you refer to it as Uncle Sam or Big Brother, the government is an 800-pound gorilla in the room with the power to levy criminal and civil charges against companies and their owners. Its unlimited resources make it an entity to avoid, even if you are confident in your innocence.

Top Takeaways From Chapter 4:

- Even if you are innocent, the government, as a potential plaintiff with unlimited resources and the power to levy criminal and civil charges against companies and their owners, is an extremely expensive adversary.

- Sales and use taxes are a growing concern for businesses, and companies should perform a nexus study to determine whether registration with the Department of Revenue in other states is necessary.

- The federal government can sue businesses for violating foreign sales and export restrictions. Companies must have a compliance program covering these regulations.

- Data privacy violations and security breaches can result in substantial costs and fines from both state and federal governments.

- Industry and company-specific laws and regulations vary across multiple levels of government, and a proactive approach to compliance can help safeguard your business from expensive fines, legal fees, and reputational harm.

Aside from the criminal/civil dichotomy, regulations applicable to businesses, business owners, and employees of businesses come at the state, federal, and local levels through a vast network of bureaucrats, agencies, and departments. These entities can utilize legislation and regulations to impose costly and burdensome proceedings and investigations against businesses and their owners. In short, the tentacles of our political system reach far and wide, and the best thing you can do as a business owner or decision-maker is to think ahead.

To prepare for potential legal challenges, business owners should instruct their attorneys annually to analyze general and industry-specific defenses and anticipate enforcement actions from the different levels and agencies of government. These agencies can include (and your lawyer should consider) the attorney general, the Federal Trade Commission (FTC), and state consumer protection agencies. Compliance with employment law alone requires anticipating the activity of the Occupational Safety and Health Administration (OSHA) for workplace safety, the Wage and Hour Division of the Department of Labor (DOL) for minimum wage, overtime, and recordkeeping, the Equal Employment Opportunity Commission (EEOC) for employment discrimination, the National Labor Relations Board (NLRB) for unionized companies, the Employee Benefits Security Administration (EBSA) for ERISA and employee benefits, and state and local agencies. Your industry may implicate additional agencies to consider, and their regulations should also be part of any compliance checklist.

Additionally, criminal laws and income tax rules enforced by the IRS, as well as sales and use tax rules overseen by State Departments of Revenue, apply universally. Your business lawyer should create and apply a thorough and comprehensive checklist that considers all generally and specifically applicable rules you need to follow.

Once a year, have a compliance discussion with your attorney. Have them spend 5–10 hours creating good compliance checklists for you and researching the hot-button issues that are making plaintiff's lawyers and regulators in your industry crazy at the moment. Then, appoint a compliance officer in your company to manage the checklist. That means they are periodically reviewing company operations to ensure compliance with those checklists, interviewing employees, reviewing policies and procedures and other documents, and doing spot checks on company processes. The compliance officer should then report back to your attorney, in an attorney-client privileged (i.e., confidential) communication, the results of those compliance audits while copying other key personnel in the business.

Below, we discuss the highest-risk exposure areas regarding government compliance and litigation.

Sales and Use Taxes

The collection of sales and use taxes is a growing concern for businesses. Now more than ever, states are chasing down any pocket they can find to close revenue short-falls, and they are getting increasingly aggressive in collecting taxes. Previously, companies with limited operations outside their home state only had to consider sales and use taxes in their jurisdiction. However, the definition of "transacting business" has expanded, allowing states to pursue companies with significant activity within their borders, including employees, assets, or customers. The Supreme Court's *South Dakota v. Wayfair* decision established that states could require out-of-state businesses to collect and transfer sales taxes on in-state consumer purchases, even without a physical presence in the state.[11]

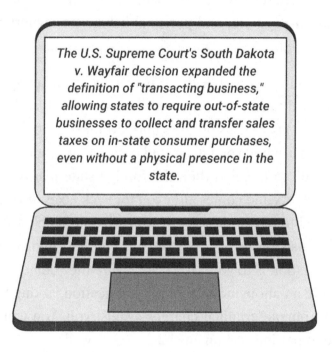

The U.S. Supreme Court's South Dakota v. Wayfair decision expanded the definition of "transacting business," allowing states to require out-of-state businesses to collect and transfer sales taxes on in-state consumer purchases, even without a physical presence in the state.

Most US companies now conduct sales beyond their state of incorporation or headquarters, creating a potentially costly area for errors. If a company has customers, employees, assets, or operations outside its home state, a nexus study can determine if registration with the Department of Revenue in other states is necessary. If so, the company may need to pay sales and use taxes and file a foreign qualification with the Department of State and Revenue.

Failure to file or keep current on tax payments can result in the foreign state pursuing back taxes, and the longer you've gone without registering or paying, the bigger that bogie can get. There may also be criminal penalties associated with non-payment, and personal liability to owners may be attached.

The good news is that there is usually an offset against your local taxes, such that you're only paying and filing taxes and tax returns on the same revenue only once. The problem is when you fall behind or don't file where you're supposed to file, and then the foreign state learns about your activity and comes after you for back taxes. If you are required to pay back taxes, it is nearly impossible to pass those costs on to your customers. The best approach in this situation is to go to the state *before* they come to you and file an anonymous amnesty application, asking them not to pursue criminal charges against you. You will still have to pay interest on any back taxes owed.

Step one is to speak to an accountant who can advise on whether you need a nexus study. Step two is to speak with a lawyer if you are already late to the party and need to file an amnesty application.

Foreign Sales

The federal government can sue your business for violating foreign sales and export restrictions. If you sell to people or entities outside the US, you must have a compliance program covering these regulations. This compliance includes ensuring you do not do business with a sanctioned country or person by cross-referencing lists from relevant authorities like the Office of Foreign Asset Control (OFAC). Failure to implement these measures may cause significant financial losses.

Data Privacy and Security

It seems like we hear about another company getting hacked almost every day. Passwords and credit card numbers are getting stolen with increasing regularity, and that's just what we know about because companies are reporting the breach. Who knows how many breaches go unreported? The government knows a lot more than we do, and they're taking data security incredibly seriously.

Violations of data security requirements can result in substantial costs and fines from both state and federal governments, making it essential to have a compliance program in place. The European Union ushered in an era of heightened scrutiny for corporations in this area with the passage of the General Data Protection Regulation (GDPR). California was quick to follow. The federal government and other states are falling quickly in line.

Government Funding Compliance

Your compliance program should monitor adherence to the relevant laws if your company receives government funding or has conducted business with state or federal entities. Government funding fraud encompasses many activities beyond just Medicare and Medicaid, so it is wise to consult a knowledgeable attorney to ensure compliance.

Failure to implement an adequate compliance program can result in severe consequences for your business, including legal action and damage to your reputation. Be sure to prioritize compliance efforts and keep them up to date to avoid potential legal action from the government.

> FAILURE TO IMPLEMENT AN ADEQUATE COMPLIANCE PROGRAM CAN RESULT IN SEVERE CONSEQUENCES FOR YOUR BUSINESS, INCLUDING LEGAL ACTION AND DAMAGE TO YOUR REPUTATION.

Industry and Company-Specific Laws and Regulations and More on Compliance Systems

Once you confirm that you're not breaking any generally applicable federal, state, and local laws, rules, and regulations, whether civil or criminal, have your attorney conduct industry and company-specific compliance research. In the US, various industries are heavily regulated, such as nursing homes, hospitals, restaurants, car dealerships, cannabis companies, energy, law, accounting, and insurance companies. Identify the relevant department or agency regulating your industry, which could be at the state, federal, or local level or across multiple levels of government.

As stated above, your attorney should tailor your compliance checklist to your industry and company. Among other things, the record-keeping from the self-audits will assist if and when the agency comes knocking on your door. On that day, you'll be able to show the regulator that you are in full compliance with their regulations. Appointing and training a good, detail-oriented compliance officer to perform regular compliance audits and procedures, with correct written documentation of the audits being performed, will further strengthen compliance. This person should correct written policies and procedures to demonstrate transparency, specificity, and clarity, leaving no room for doubt by employees, supervisors, and regulators as to whether you are or are not complying with the rules.

To help you in this process, we've included materials in the bonus chapter, Audit Thyself, on performing Self-Audits, and there is a compliance program checklist in Appendix M (see p. 225).

After implementing a compliance system, your attorney should perform industry- and agency-specific research into recent hot-button enforcement issues that apply to you to identify potential issues and areas for improvement. Who is the attorney general in your state going after, and for what violations? Who is your regulator? What kinds of practices have ticked off their office recently? What do you need to do to stay off their radar, and what do they need to see to be satisfied if you end up on it? That's the conversation you should be having with your attorney about government enforcement. After that conversation, have all work products put into written advice and documentation and then follow it.

A proactive approach to compliance can help safeguard your business from expensive fines, legal fees, and reputational harm.

>>>>> <<<<<

Governments ensure that business owners are not gaining an unfair competitive advantage by enforcing compliance with regulations. Similarly, business competitors also monitor each other's compliance. In the next chapter, we will delve into the topic of how business competitors may take legal action against each other and how they may infringe on each other's rights.

Chapter 5: Competitors

A RE YOU INFRINGING ON your competitors' rights, or are they infringing on yours? Is there any infringement at all? Let's examine how to conduct business ethically and avoid legal disputes with your competitors.

Top Takeaways From Chapter 5:

- Conduct intellectual property (IP) audits periodically because a defensive IP approach can be more costly than an offensive approach.

- Seek the guidance of an IP attorney to protect your IP rights adequately.

- Restrictive covenants protect your company's confidential information and trade secrets from current or future competitors.

- There are four main types of restrictive covenants: confidentiality agreements, non-poaching agreements, non-solicitation agreements, and non-competition agreements. Each has its pros and cons and applicability.

- Businesses should conduct an analysis to determine whether they possess any confidential or proprietary information that could be detrimental if it were to be disclosed to competitors or made public.

- Confidentiality agreements will not protect your information if it is already public or becomes public.

- Non-compete agreements are generally the most difficult of all restrictive covenants to enforce.

Intellectual Property

Intellectual property claims encompass patents, trademarks, or copyrights that are in play in your business.

Seek the guidance of an IP attorney to protect those rights adequately.

Offensive

From an offensive standpoint, your IP attorney can advise you on what trademarks, copyrights, and patents you should acquire from the US Patent and Trademark Office, from a private party, or by other means to safeguard your assets.

Offensively, you can safeguard your intellectual properties in the following ways:

- Patents protect your rights to your inventions.

- Trademarks protect your "marks" (i.e., your names, logos, brand, and goodwill).

- Copyrights protect your other expressed creative works.

Defensive

Defensively, you should know whether you are at risk of infringing a competitor's IP. You should also consider alternative IP strategies short of application and acquisition, such as licensing and strategic partnerships.

Sometimes, infringement can happen unknowingly. That will not let you off the hook. A court can still hold you liable for damages and force you to stop using, selling, or distributing the products at issue.

IP Audits

Conduct IP audits regularly. Your lawyers should perform thorough research and analysis to ensure your business operations do not infringe on another business's IP rights.

IP audits can save you a lot of money. One of the costliest legal battles we ever faced was defending our client against a patent troll's claims in federal court. Although victorious, our victory came with a $300,000 legal fee price tag. Had we performed an IP audit upfront, we would have discussed getting intellectual property insurance coverage or creating workarounds that were even more obvious than the ones we had (and ultimately won the case with). We might have also considered a patent strategy whereby we proactively went to the patent market and obtained, purchased, or licensed patents to cover us in that situation. Unfortunately, our defensive approach was more costly than an offensive approach.

Whether it's an offensive or defensive analysis, an analysis of intellectual property potential and opportunities, rights, and obligations is always a good idea. These can cost a few thousand dollars, or they can cost a few hundred thousand dollars. There is generally going to be an 80-20 analysis that fits into your budget, the size and kind of company and product that you have, and the industry that you're in, as well as the competitors that you have.

Restrictive Covenants

One area where intellectual property and employment co-incide is restrictive covenants with your employees. These documents are there, among other reasons, to protect your confidential information and trade secrets from current and future competitors (who may be your current employees).

Experienced lawyers can draft one of these four main types of restrictive covenants:

1. Confidentiality agreements (generally the easiest to enforce)

2. Non-employee poaching agreements

3. Non-solicitation agreements

4. Non-competition agreements (generally the hardest to enforce

The enforceability and scope of re-strictive covenants vary depending on the state and industry. Different states and industries have their own specific rules. Generally, we recommend businesses conduct an analysis to determine whether they

THE ENFORCEABILITY AND SCOPE OF RESTRICTIVE COVENANTS VARY DEPENDING ON THE STATE AND INDUSTRY.

possess any economically valuable nonpublic and confi-dential and/or proprietary information within their busi-nesses that could be detrimental if it were to be disclosed to competitors or made public. Most businesses have some kind of confidential information they want to protect that falls into one or more of these categories: trade secrets, proprietary processes, or intellectual property.

The analysis to identify and protect this information should follow these steps:

- First, identify what confidential information your business has that fits the above categories.

- Next, take active steps to protect it. These steps should include both physical and electronic lock-and-key security mechanisms, need-to-know distribution limitations, security policies and pro-cedures, and confidentiality agreements with em-ployees and third parties with access to the infor-mation.

Confidentiality Agreements

Confidentiality agreements will not protect you if the information is already public or becomes public. As a general matter, we advise our clients to have these in place with all of their employees. If there is any confidential information in the business (and there usually is), when the employee leaves the business disgruntled or is causing damage to your business in some way, the confidentiality agreement may often come into play as a hook to have a court prevent your former employee from causing damage to your company.

In many cases, your employees will not be able to afford a lawyer at that time or want to avoid the headache of going through litigation with you. A cease and desist letter or transmission to them of a draft complaint for their disclosure of confidential information may be just the kind of weapon that gets them to play nice.

Non-poaching and Non-solicitation Agreements

Non-poaching and non-solicitation agreements prohibit employees from soliciting or poaching clients or other employees from the company. They are generally more difficult to enforce than confidentiality agreements but can still be effective when appropriately drafted. Drafters should narrowly tailor these agreements to the specific circumstances of your business and the employees involved.

For instance, it may be difficult to prevent an employee from contacting a client post-employment if they never had contact with or awareness of that client while they worked for you. On the other hand, it may be easier to enforce an agreement that prevents employees who worked with a client while employed by your business from contacting that client post-employment.

Non-competition Agreements

A non-compete agreement is a contract between an employer and an employee that restricts the employee from working for a competitor or starting a competing business for a specific time. They can be critical when dealing with senior executives with access to highly confidential information and have played a key role in building the company's client base and operations. These agreements protect the value created through the investment in that employee but are the most difficult to enforce.

Aside from enforcement difficulty, non-competition agreements are also becoming increasingly unpopular. Courts

CONSULT WITH A LAWYER BEFORE USING A NON-COMPETE.

and legislatures, as a matter of public policy, want people to have the freedom to work where they choose and put food on the table, pay taxes, buy homes, and send their kids to college. The Federal Trade Commission has expressed skepticism about their enforceability, and California largely prohibits them. That doesn't mean you shouldn't use them. It just means you should discuss them with counsel and use them surgically in an enforceable way.

Non-compete enforceability is generally easier when the scope, geography, and time limit are narrow and when the employee in question is a higher-level company employee. Enforceability is also easier in business-to-business or shareholder contexts than with individual employees or customers.

The conversation with your lawyer should focus on the extent to which a non-compete agreement is advisable and would be enforceable against certain employees in your company. After you invest in the relationship, disclose highly confidential information to them, and build the client base and the operation with them to yield high ROI value and business results from your investment, you want to do whatever you can to prevent your senior vice president from taking your business and robbing it of that value that you created together.

Advertising and Defamation

It is not uncommon for competitors to attack each other through claims of false advertising or other unfair competition. The Lanham Act empowers private parties to protect their interests and goodwill from such behavior. Claims under the Lanham Act refer to false or misleading advertising that can hold competitors liable for creating confusion about the origin of goods and services, such as palming off one's goods and services as a competitor's product.

Under the Lanham Act, you can also sue a competitor for false or misleading statements that misrepresent your product or service, including those related to product quality, pricing, or any other business aspect. Even technically accurate but misleading advertising by competitors is actionable.

Implied statements in advertisements are actionable under the Lanham Act. For example, an ad that claims "no product purer than XYZ Product" may not initially seem like false or misleading advertising. But if the ad features an unnamed comparison product with the same coloring or markings as your product, you could argue that the ad implies your product is impure, constituting false advertising.

The Lanham Act only allows legal action against certain types of statements. Statements of opinion, truthful negative statements, and puffery are not actionable. Puffery refers to exaggerated praise, such as a neon sign proclaiming "Best XYZ Product in Town." The Lanham Act aims to prevent companies from gaining an unfair market advantage through false or misleading information rather than simple exaggeration.

Conduct an audit with your lawyer to assess the potential for a claim of unfair competition resulting from your advertising, social media, or statements made by your salespeople or employees.

⋙ ⋘

Protecting your business's confidential information is crucial to maintaining a competitive advantage and preventing harm to your company.

An equally crucial consideration is how your employees may be litigation risks for your company. We will explore this topic in the next chapter.

PROTECTING YOUR BUSINESS'S CONFIDENTIAL INFORMATION IS CRUCIAL TO MAINTAINING A COMPETITIVE ADVANTAGE AND PREVENTING HARM TO YOUR COMPANY.

Chapter 6: Employees

E MPLOYEES GENERALLY REPRESENT THE smallest group of plaintiffs (unless you're a very large employer). The problem is that this small group has the largest number of potential claims. Each has layers and layers of obligations you owe under state, federal, local, or industry rules, regulations, and laws.

This chapter explores employees as a plaintiff class and how to protect your company from them and their lawyers, many of whom are aggressive contingency fee lawyers who take cases with questionable merit simply to squeeze companies for fees. (Pro tip: if some areas of the law have lots of lawyers who practice only in that one area and do it for a percentage of their recovery, you need to really beef up that part of your fort. Employment law is one such area.)

Top Takeaways From Chapter 6:

- Businesses should invest in a detailed, industry-specific handbook drafted specifically for their operations by an employment attorney. The upfront investment will save significant litigation costs down the road.

- The handbook should include non-negotiable items such as an at-will employment policy, an explicit non-discrimination policy, an outline of how to handle discrimination complaints, and a waterfall dispute provision.

- The handbooks should also include policies on leaves of absence (FMLA), workplace substance use and testing, zero-tolerance workplace violence, weapons on the premises, workplace equipment use, and confidentiality.

- Employees should sign an acknowledgment that they have read and understood the employee handbook.

- The handbook will only be effective if it is enforced. Set up an internal policy and process to review and enforce handbook policies and then enforce that policy and process.

- Companies with manufacturing or safety issues must pay attention to OSHA—the Occupational Safety and Health Administration. OSHA regulations should be added to your compliance checklist, if applicable.

- The Fair Labor Standards Act (FLSA) describes the employees who are exempt or non-exempt from overtime pay. To ensure FLSA compliance, employee job descriptions must be accurate and indicate their exemption or non-exemption status.

Over the past two decades, employee lawsuits have increased by about 400%, with wrongful termination lawsuits alone rising by over 260%.[12] The cost of settling employment claims out of court averages around $40,000. In a 2017 study of 1,214 closed employment claims involving businesses with fewer than five hundred employees, 24% of claims resulted in defense and settlement costs averaging $160,000.[13] Plaintiffs in employment discrimination cases can pursue remedies, including front pay, back pay, and compensatory and punitive damages. Even businesses with 15–100 employees may face awards of up to $50,000 for compensatory and punitive damages alone. Attorney and expert fees for plaintiffs are also potential remedies.[14] Pause there: paying for the attorneys' fees for both sides exponentially increases the cost of defense and overall exposure. Complying with state, federal, local, or industry obligations, regulations, and laws is essential for avoiding these lengthy, expensive, and painful claims. Implementing a checklist-based compliance program is the best way to maintain adequate protection.

Your compliance checklist will vary based on your employees' work environments, including safety requirements, overtime and personnel record reporting requirements, and industry and state standards. To maintain compliance and minimize the risk of employee lawsuits, have your lawyer prepare a checklist reviewed for each employee when they start and annually for all employees.

Handbook Policies and Procedures

All businesses with at least five employees should have a well-crafted employee handbook that clearly articulates their employment policies in writing (though there really is no minimum number of employees that would yield the benefit of having a handbook). This is the easiest way to communicate expectations and clear misunderstandings to avoid litigation. The handbook and policies can be electronic, but your employees should sign a separate document stating that they have received, reviewed, understood, had the ability to ask questions, and will comply with all of your standards as set forth in the handbook and any separate written employment policies and procedures. This method may seem obvious, but in our experience, most companies need to pay more attention to drafting, auditing, and updating their handbooks.

Needless to say, drafting an effective employee handbook should not be a DIY process. I can't tell you how often our clients have gotten into hot wa-

> A WELL-DRAFTED HANDBOOK CAN SAVE YOU FROM THE COST OF LITIGATION.

ter using a generic employee handbook pulled off of Google or obtained from their payroll company. Your payroll company does not understand your business and probably uses the same template for all of their clients. Aside from being overgeneralized, it also may not comply with state and federal laws applicable to your business.

We highly recommend that your employment lawyer customize your handbook and policies for your business. Depending on your company's size and complexity, expect to spend between $2,500 and $10,000. This cost is a fraction of what you would pay in legal fees after getting sued. It is an investment worth making to minimize your risk of exposure.

Contents

Your employee handbook must make clear that you do not discriminate based on any protected class and should have a process set forth for reporting any complaints of discrimination or harassment.

State confidentiality or non-solicitation obligations in separate agreements that are tailored to each position in the company. (For example, all employees should sign confidentiality agreements, but most employees should not necessarily sign non-competition agreements.)

At the very least, your handbook should include:

- Language stating that employees are at-will and can be hired or fired for any reason that is not against public policy.

- An explicit statement that your company does not discriminate based on membership in any protected class, including but not limited to race, gender, national origin, religion, etc.

- An outline of a clear process for reporting any complaints of discrimination or harassment.

- A five-part waterfall dispute resolution document, if enforceable, based on your industry and geographic choice of law. If it is, have one similar to what you would have with a customer, supplier, or owner. (See Chapter 1.)

Regarding alternate dispute resolution, under the recently enacted Ending Forced Arbitration of Sexual Assault and Sexual Harassment Act, you cannot compel arbitration of any employment-related sexual harassment or sexual discrimination claims. Your employee handbook should include a carve-out for these claims instead of relying on mediation alone to resolve them.

Once you have established your compliance program, as outlined in this and the government chapter, you may incorporate those requirements into your handbook or policies and procedures. The employee handbook is typically a shorter document, while policies and procedures and compliance standards tend to be longer, more complex documents that apply differently to various departments within your company. Keeping these documents separate but coordinated can provide far more comprehensive guidance and protection for your business than an employee handbook alone.

> KEEPING THESE DOCUMENTS SEPARATE BUT COORDINATED CAN PROVIDE FAR MORE COMPREHENSIVE GUIDANCE AND PROTECTION FOR YOUR BUSINESS THAN AN EMPLOYEE HANDBOOK ALONE.

Non-discrimination and Equal Employment Opportunity Statements

Title VII of the Civil Rights Act of 1964 established the Equal Employment Opportunity Commission to enforce employment discrimination laws, prohibiting discrimination based on race, color, religion, sex, or national origin. To promote fair employment practices, businesses should explicitly state in their employee handbooks and also in employment applications that they do not discriminate based on any protected class and provide a clear process for reporting discrimination or harassment. Such policies can decrease the likelihood of discriminatory behavior by employees and demonstrate the company's commitment to non-discrimination.

The other reason to have these policies expressed in writing is to provide an initial argument that when an employee discriminates against another employee, she is doing so in violation of company policy. This is an important barrier of liability between the employer company and the discriminating employee, so long as the company takes action to prevent and remedy the discrimination immediately.

Leave of Absence Policies

The Family Medical Leave Act requires businesses with fifty or more employees to provide eligible employees with up to twelve workweeks of unpaid leave. Compliance with the FMLA can be difficult due to its varying rules. Communicate a clear action plan to employees regarding eligibility, how to request a leave of absence, and the duration of the leave.

Even if your business is not covered under the FMLA, implementing a leave of absence policy can clarify the process for taking unpaid time off for circumstances such as medical issues, jury duty, military duties, pregnancy, and childbirth. Additionally, the Uniformed Services Employment and Reemployment Rights Act of 1994 requires employers to grant unpaid leave to military service members.

Illegal Substances and Alcohol-Free Workplace and Testing Policies

To ensure a safe and productive workplace, it is recommended that businesses speak with their counsel about implementing certain drug-free workplace programs to prevent hazardous conditions caused by employee intoxication. Regardless of an employer's views on recreational drugs, a policy prohibiting their use *on the job* is a bare minimum. Any such use would, therefore, be a violation of company policy, and assuming enforcement of that policy, the employer has an argument that the employee was "on a lark" and broke clearly spelled-out rules when she caused damage to the plaintiff. This argument is not foolproof, but the policy has weight and may deter such behavior in the first place.

An Illegal Substances and Alcohol-Free Workplace and Testing Policy should be added to the employee handbook and job posting to clearly communicate the company's stance on drug and alcohol use in the workplace and when drug testing may be required. The policy should also state that the use of over-the-counter and prescription medication to treat a disability is not prohibited.

If drug testing is conducted, it should be done in an objective, uniform, and non-discriminatory way with minimal intrusiveness, and the information gathered should be kept private to avoid violating employee privacy rights.

Zero-Tolerance Workplace Violence Policy

Employers must ensure a safe workplace under the Occupational Safety and Health Act's Section 5(a)(1), which includes taking action to prevent workplace violence. OSHA advises adopting a zero-tolerance workplace violence policy, which can be used to defend against an OSHA violation claim.

The policy should specify immediate termination for anyone who engages in workplace violence. This measure reduces the risk of negligent retention or supervision claims and helps keep your employees safe.

Weapons Restrictions

To promote workplace safety, adopt a policy that restricts or prohibits concealed weapons. The policy should define which weapons are restricted or prohibited, the restrictions or prohibitions imposed on those weapons, whether you will provide a place for storage of the restricted or prohibited weapons, provide procedures for investigating violations of the policy, and instruct employees to report any actual or suspected violations of the policy.

Equipment Use and Reimbursement Guidelines

If your business permits employees to use company-owned equipment like computers, printers, or cell phones, it's important to protect your business from potential damage to this equipment. To do so, require employees to sign an Equipment Use Agreement that specifies which equipment they are assigned, mandates reimbursement for any damages caused to the equipment, and documents the dates on which the equipment was issued and returned. Your employee handbook should include this agreement.

Other Considerations: Confidentiality and Non-solicitation Considerations

To ensure confidentiality and non-solicitation obligations, it's best to protect these matters in separate agreements. Whether to include confidentiality provisions in the employee handbook should be decided on a case-by-case basis after consulting your business lawyer. Securing separate signed agreements is the best practice for protecting this information, though confidentiality provisions may often be inserted into both handbooks and separate agreements.

Acknowledgment

As previously mentioned, your handbook can be physical or electronic, but employees should sign a separate, physical document acknowledging their review, understanding, and compliance with the standards outlined in the handbook and any written policies and procedures.

Compliance

Once a seasoned employment attorney expertly crafts your employee handbook and written policies and procedures, your work is not complete. It is wise to document your standards, but it is foolish to have them documented and not put them into practice. You must do both.

If you have an HR manager, it would be her responsibility to ensure compliance. If not, consider outsourcing your HR function to a third party that can oversee adherence to your written policies, procedures, and handbooks. If you don't want to hire an HR manager or outsource that responsibility, you must appoint and train someone inside the company to ensure compliance with your standards.

Consistency is the key attribute you must have when implementing and enforcing your handbook policies and procedures. Enforce all policies with all employees in your organization without exception, or they can use deviations as evidence of discrimination.

Hot Button Issues: OSHA and FLSA

Occupational Safety and Health Administration (OSHA)

Companies with manufacturing or safety concerns must pay attention to OSHA—the Occupational Safety and

Health Administration. This should be a separate item on your compliance checklist. OSHA is a federal agency that sets and enforces workplace safety standards nationwide. Its main goal is to ensure workers have a safe and healthy work environment. It does this by issuing regulations, providing training and education, and conducting workplace inspections.

Employers are required to comply with OSHA standards, which cover a wide range of safety issues, including electrical hazards, machinery safety, fall protection, and hazardous materials handling.

Some of the most frequently cited standards when OSHA conducts inspections relate to the following safety issues:

- Respiratory protection

- Hazard communication

- Control of hazardous energy (lockout/tagout)

- Powered industrial trucks

- Machine guarding[15]

The construction business faces some of the most-cited OSHA violations, including safety risks from fall protection (or lack thereof) and training, ladders, scaffolding, and eye and face protection.

OSHA standards vary depending on the industry and type of work being performed. Across the board, OSHA requires employers to keep records of work-related injuries and illnesses and to report severe incidents to the agency.

> OSHA REQUIRES
> EMPLOYERS TO KEEP
> RECORDS OF
> WORK-RELATED
> INJURIES AND
> ILLNESSES AND TO
> REPORT SEVERE
> INCIDENTS TO THE
> AGENCY.

Failure to comply with OSHA regulations can result in fines, penalties, and legal liability if an employee is injured or killed due to a safety violation. You can be fined up to $15,625 per violation and up to $156,259 per violation for willful or repeated violations.[16]

Adding OSHA regulations to your compliance checklist, prioritizing safety in the workplace, and staying current with OSHA regulation changes will safeguard against compliance violations and employee legal claims.

Fair Labor Standards Act (FLSA)

Liability under the FLSA is a contentious issue between employees and employers for several reasons, including views by some practitioners and employers that they create one-sided and harsh standards in overtime pay disputes. To comply with the FLSA, accurately document job descriptions for each employee, indicating their exemption or non-exemption status from the FLSA. Exemption means no obligation to pay overtime and is a designation generally reserved for senior-level managers, directors, and executives.

Exemption status for employees is not determined solely by their hourly or salaried status.

Exempt employees must meet three criteria:

1. Be a salaried employee.

2. Earn a minimum weekly salary, which is currently $684 as of January 1, 2020.

3. Fit within one of the exempt employee categories: executive, administrative, professional, computer, and outside sales employees (require independent judgment in their role).

If an employee meets these criteria, there is no obligation to pay them overtime. They are exempt. If an employee does not meet these criteria, they are non-exempt and entitled to overtime pay at time and a half for any hours worked over 40 per week. Non-exempt status typically applies to lower-ranking employees and administrative roles, such as secretaries, manufacturing floor workers, blue-collar workers, mechanics, and similar positions.

Murky job descriptions can lead to employees claiming they were misclassified and needing to be properly paid for overtime. Without proper records and policies, this can become a "he said/she said" situation where the employee is likely to win. If they win, you may have to pay punitive damages on top of time and a half, effectively doubling your damages.[17] You may also be responsible for paying their attorney fees.

The best practice is to have detailed job descriptions and a written policy that says overtime is permitted only when approved by a manager in writing. It is essential to require the manager and employee to maintain good records of the time worked every week.

These policies are crucial to ensure clarity and understanding between you and your employees. It also protects your company from potential legal claims and helps to maintain a positive relationship with your employees.

An exempt employee checklist is available in Appendix Q. (See p. 249.)

Discrimination and Family Medical Leave Act (FMLA)

The layers of state and federal laws, rules, and regulations that apply to employees can be overwhelming. Discrimination and the Family Medical Leave Act (FMLA) are examples of areas often regulated, sometimes in different ways at the state and federal levels, and sometimes with differing industry-specific regulations, further complicating compliance.

While the specifics for compliance are beyond the scope of this book, it is essential to discuss all such laws and standards with an experienced employment lawyer. Set up a compliance system to ensure that you don't slip into hot water in these areas, and make sure your compliance standards are clearly spelled out in your employee handbook and separate written policies and procedures.

See Appendix G (p. 191): FMLA Compliance Checklist for more information on this topic.

Contractors vs. Employees

Countless clients come into our office with employees who are misclassified as contractors. We get it: you want to save money on benefits and payroll taxes and compliance with sometimes-burdensome employment laws. The problem is when you get it wrong. There's a right way and a wrong way to classify your employees, and often, you can still classify certain folks as contractors *if* you document and manage the relationship correctly.

Incorrectly categorizing workers as contractors or employees, whether intentionally or mistakenly, can cause massive problems with the IRS and the Department of Labor. Taking someone who is doing the same tasks as an employee and making them a contractor to avoid paying them benefits is generally a bad idea and can result in significant fines and penalties.

If an employer misclassifies an employee as an independent contractor, they may be subject to legal consequences and penalties, including back taxes, fines, and lawsuits. There are ways, however, to meet the company's fair objectives the right way. If you're going to classify somebody as a contractor, then they should have a contract in writing that an experienced attorney creates. You can do this fairly easily by providing a written contract that includes:

- A detailed description of the services

- A clear evaluation standard

- Dispute resolution provisions

- Confidentiality obligations

- Non-disparagement clauses

- A statement that the contractor is not an agent, employee, or joint venturer of the business

It is not enough to include a contract clause stating that the contractor is an independent contractor. Many business owners simply rely on that language foolishly. It is essential for employers to correctly determine whether a worker is an independent contractor or an employee based on the characteristics of the worker's relationship with your business. This designation is vital because it impacts several important areas of legal compliance, including payroll taxes, benefits, and labor laws.

Independent contractors are self-employed individuals who offer their services to businesses and have more control over their work schedules. They are responsible for paying their own taxes, insurance, and other expenses.

Employees work under an employer's direction and control and are entitled to certain rights and protections, such as minimum wage, overtime pay, and worker's compensation benefits.

To determine whether a worker is an independent contractor or an employee, employers must consider various factors.

- The degree of control the employer has over the worker and the time, place, and manner of their performance of the work.

- The worker's ability to make a profit or suffer a loss.

- The permanency of the working relationship.

- The extent to which the worker provides their own tools and equipment.

Employers should consult with legal counsel to ensure they correctly classify their workers and comply with applicable laws and regulations.

We recommend asking your contractor to consider having an LLC, although you may want the owner of the LLC to guarantee the contract. They should also get insurance naming you as an additional insured or named insured on the policy. That contract can then have all of the other bells and whistles you would have in any other contract, including a good dispute resolution clause, confidentiality, non-disparagement, and so on.

More information is available on this topic in Appendix R: Employees vs Independent Contractors. (See p. 259.)

Employment Practices Liability Insurance (EPLI)

It is important to pause and remember what this book is all about: How to stay out of court and avoid costly legal battles. One of the most effective ways to do this is by obtaining Employment Practices Liability Insurance, commonly called EPLI coverage.

> INVESTING IN EPLI COVERAGE DEMONSTRATES A PROACTIVE COMMITMENT TO PROTECTING YOUR EMPLOYEES AND YOUR BUSINESS.

A common misconception is that general liability insurance or business liability insurance will cover claims brought by employees, but these policies often exclude such claims. We are often surprised at how frequently businesses with a significant number of employees fail to have adequate EPLI coverage in place. This can be a costly mistake for any business.

EPLI protects against various employee-related claims that can result in significant financial losses and damage to a business, such as wrongful termination, harassment, discrimination, and retaliation.

In addition to providing financial protection, it can help prevent lawsuits. Businesses can significantly reduce the likelihood of employee claims by implementing strong policies and procedures and providing comprehensive employee training.[18]

Conclusion

Y OU'VE JUST READ ABOUT the universe of plaintiffs and how to build a six-sided fortress around your business. We've done our best to condense decades of law practice into this short book for you. You've received a lot of talking points for your next meeting with your business attorney. We hope this quick read helped you understand the many areas of exposure to litigation that business owners face and what they can do about those risk areas.

The following pages are additional resources to bolster your business, safeguard your processes, and keep you out of court. We invite you to take our free assessment at our CoverMySix website, covermysix.com , so you can receive your customized risk report. Taking this report, book, and appendices into your lawyer's office will save you thousands of dollars, hours, and headaches.

We look forward to hearing how you grow your business and cover your six.

Bonus Chapter: Audit Thyself: How to Conduct an Internal Audit

T HE BEST WAY TO be proactive vs. reactive is to conduct a good, old-fashioned internal audit. It's tough, it's time-consuming, but it's worth it.

Here's how you do it:

Step 1: Create a written plan.

- Use a Gantt chart that shows you a visual, calendar-style depiction of *who's* doing *what* and *when*.

- Your plan or Gantt chart will specify all the tasks in the audit, name the person responsible for each task, and state how long that task will go from a start date to an end date.

- Do online research for Gantt charts or some combination of "internal audit Gantt chart," and you'll see what others have done.

Step 2: Identify the universe of legal exposure areas that your company is likely to have.

- Picture your company as a leaky bucket and try to figure out what's likely to cause those leaks.

- Another image I like to use is something Tony Robbins uses: a car or bike wheel divided into pie pieces radiating outwards from the center, with each pie only going out as far as the company is compliant in that area. When one pie piece is shorter than the other ones (because, for example, hiring practices are 60% compliant while most of the other areas are 90% compliant), your car or bike is going to have a bumpy ride.

- Usually, the exposure areas (or pie pieces) fall into these categories: employment, tax, corporate, contracts, government regulation, real estate, and information technology/security.

Step 3: Get specific.

- Drill down into those leaky areas to the ones specific to your business. This is where talking to a lawyer helps.

- Lawyers can issue-spot. For example, on the employment piece of your bucket/wheel, your business lawyer will ask you if you have independent contractors. If you do, one of the drill-down areas will be the proper classification of contractors and employees. Another issue your business lawyer will spot is proper exemption classification. It's hard to spot those issues if you're not a lawyer.

- Lawyers are more likely to be objective. Business owners are like parents of small children or writers of crappy novels. They think their creations are better, smarter, or more interesting than they actually are.

- Lawyers audit confidentially because of attorney-client privilege. With few exceptions, you can protect your compliance audit and all the nasty cobwebs it uncovers with a confidentiality that may be far stronger than any non-disclosure agreement you've signed with your employees.

- Lawyers create more specific compliance areas based on the type of business you run and the facts and circumstances inside your business. If you're a manufacturer or a car dealership, one specific area within the government regulation pie may be OSHA compliance or environmental compliance. If you're a retailer, one specific area under government compliance may be FTC (Federal Trade Commission) or CSPA (Consumer Sales Practices Act) compliance.

- If your lawyer is not involved, you may be able to get close by looking up "Ohio employment compliance areas," "[your state] safety compliance," or "[your industry] government regulations." Spend a lot of time on this and try to create a hierarchy of compliance areas as best as you can.

Step 4: Create a compliance checklist for each area.

Creating good checklists is important. Whether you do or do not use a lawyer, don't expect a perfect checklist or a perfect audit. The goal is to plug big leaks, the ones that either draw the most attention from plaintiffs' lawyers and government agencies, have the highest rates of investigation, have the highest exposure points, and the ones that will cost you the most if you get it wrong. Your business will also have its own priorities.

- Start with Pareto's Principle: What are the 20% of compliance issues that tend to be responsible for 80% of the exposure?

- Expand that to 30 or 40% until you can account for 90–95% of the exposure points in terms of liability and expense.

- Prioritize your drill-down areas and checklist items into high-, medium-, and low-risk items, and note them as such on the checklist.

- Later, when you create a report card, you'll use weighted values to create a sliding scale of scores based on the risk level of each item.

This is probably more art than science, but you're unlikely to create a 100% compliant company without making the audit process more of a pain than it's worth.

Step 5: Create your team.

Choose your team wisely, assign tasks, and then meet with them to explain. Employee communications should be on a need-to-know basis. Let employees not involved in the audit go about their business and lives without worrying about what an audit might mean.

When we prepare to do an audit for our clients, we have an introductory call or meeting with managers at various tiers of the company who will be involved in the audit. Managing communications is important to avoid panic or anxiety. We tell managers that this is intended to help the company keep more of its money and stay out of trouble, nothing more. We tell them it's not intended to embarrass or punish anyone, solely to identify and fix legal issues. They tend to be receptive to this message.

We also talk about confidentiality, candor, and integrity of the process. This is important and should be carefully scripted.

Step 6: Document requests and spot-checking.

- Send a document request to the people in your company most likely to have relevant documents. If you get any pushback, you're probably on to something.

- Review the documents closely against the checklist items specific to the documents.

- If you're in a regulated industry, there are probably disclosure obligations or magic language about privacy or warranties or something similar. They often need to match the regulations verbatim.

- Many of your document requests will involve spot-checking. Sometimes, you'll want to send someone trustworthy to file locations to pull their own documents. For checklist items that don't involve documents (for example, is there a proper eye washing station in your garage bay, if one is required), you, your lawyer, or your designee will physically go to the department to observe compliance or non-compliance.

Step 7: Conduct interviews.

This is necessary to learn about processes and practices difficult to read in a document or observe when spot-checking. Use the "funnel technique." Start with open-ended questions and then drill down to the compliance checklist items, veering off when you hear something worthy of a detour. If you're delegating to managers, coach them on how to conduct proper interviews.

Step 8: Make written findings.

At this point, you're going to generate a report. Ideally, your checklist was specific enough to tell you what was necessary to comply or not comply. Your findings should reference those items.

Step 9: Create a report card.

Here, you'll grade your compliance and non-compliance. Use grades like in school. They are easy to administer and give businesses goals to strive for in the next go-round. Remember, not all compliance areas are equal, and not all checklist items within those compliance areas are equal. Having an employee handbook with strict anti-discrimination policies and having the right labor law posters on the wall may be more important than ensuring that your vacation policy has been properly communicated to that one remote employee you have in Alaska.

Step 10: Create a fix-it report.

Once you've identified your leaks, create a new checklist to plug them. This is often a copy/paste job from your report card. Start with the high-dollar/high-risk items and work your way down, flagging any show-stoppers. Assign each fix to a particular manager and create a new Gantt chart that says who is doing what and when.

Step 11: Follow up.

You're almost there. Don't waste all that effort. You need to follow up on the fixes to make sure they're getting done, and then you need to do a periodic follow-up on the entire audit to make sure no one's sloughing off and that your car is still running on a smooth wheel. We recommend revisiting your audit at least every six months, at the very least, on the high-dollar items. Revisit your checklists once a year to ensure that new regulations haven't created new compliance areas or new individual checklist items.

Bonus Chapter: How to Hire a Lawyer: A Guide to Saving Money on Legal Fees

T HIS GUIDE IS DESIGNED to help you find the right lawyer and educate you on some of the realities of the legal marketplace, with a focus on how to save money on legal fees.

First, you need to understand that there are a lot of lawyers out there. The legal profession has always been saturated, with more lawyers entering the profession than leaving it. This means that there are a lot of lawyers who don't know what they're doing, and they all seem to have good advertising. Ignore the advertising. The upside to the large pool of lawyers is that you can shop around, and you will find good quality lawyers in the marketplace if you know where to look and how to work with them.

Location

Location matters when it comes to legal fees. Hiring a lawyer with a large office downtown in a big city will generally cost more than hiring the same lawyer with a small office in the suburbs. Similarly, hiring a lawyer from a large law firm will likely cost more than hiring the same lawyer from a smaller firm. Specialized lawyers also tend to charge more than general practitioners.

None of this is intended to steer you away from hiring a big-city, specialized lawyer at a large firm. In some cases, these lawyers may be necessary. But often, you can find qualified, expert legal counsel without driving downtown. If you're reading this book, a downtown, big-firm lawyer will likely be a waste of money because CoverMySix is designed to greatly reduce your risk of litigation in the first place.

Fee Negotiation

In most cases, legal fees are negotiable. You have more power than you realize. You just need to know how to use it. Just because a lawyer quotes an hourly rate of $350 or $500 or requests a $20,000 retainer does not mean you have to pay that amount. You can and should negotiate and counteroffer.

Here is how to negotiate fees:

1. ALWAYS ask for a budget. And if they tell you they can't give you one, walk out the door. Never sign an engagement letter without a well-reasoned and properly tightened budget. While the lawyer may add caveats

and disclaimers, they should be willing to work with you to keep costs within the budget.

Think of your lawyer as a glorified waterproofing company. If you had a flooded basement, a waterproofing company would send someone to assess the situation and provide an estimate for the cost of repairs. If they could not provide a reasonable estimate or insisted on billing you by the hour, you would not hire them. Your lawyer should be treated the same way. With your waterproofer, plumber, or roofer, you would take multiple bids, and you would ask for firm budgets. You should do the same with the lawyer that you're going to hire, especially if you're going to spend tens or hundreds of thousands of dollars.

2. If a lawyer tells you they bill by the hour, after you get a budget, ask if they will bill you at a capped fee. This means you do not have to go beyond a specified amount or a flat fee.

3. Ask the lawyer if they would bill you on a contingency basis or a hybrid hourly and contingency basis if they are representing you in a plaintiff capacity, meaning that you are going to sue somebody for infringing your rights, and there is an upside for you. Then, the lawyer, if they are smart and willing to partner with you, may consider sharing the risk with you by taking some of their fees on an hourly basis and some of their fee on a percentage or

success basis. Savvy lawyers do this because risk-sharing is also highly profitable if done properly.

4. When you have a lot of legal work to assign or a significant legal matter that will cost at least $50,000 or more, consider using an RFP (request for proposals) process. Don't hesitate to ask for bids from lawyers just like you would for other services, like when your roof needs fixing.

   a. Use the RFP process to ask important questions, like how the lawyer will staff your case, their experience with cases like yours, how much they will bill you, and their anticipated budget and strategy.

   b. Consider adding any additional questions that you feel are relevant.

   c. If a lawyer feels that responding to an RFP is beneath them, or if they act high and mighty towards you, it may not be a good fit for a long-term working relationship. Choose a lawyer who understands that you are a businessperson making a business decision and recognizes that you are using finite resources to solve a major problem in your life.

Engagement Letter

The engagement letter is how law firms generally present their one-sided contract provisions to their clients. Ninety-nine percent of the time, clients sign the engagement letter without questioning these provisions. Clients are either unaware of their ability to negotiate or respond intelligently to that engagement letter or are simply afraid to do so because they are feeling vulnerable and inferior in intellect and expertise relative to the lawyer. Clients just want the problem to go away, and they don't want to insult the lawyer. But if questioning a one-sided or unfair engagement letter offends them, you should offend them.

Here's some advice when it comes to the engagement letter:

1. Read every word!

2. Often, lawyers try to waive a future conflict of interest; don't let them do that.

3. Instead of having them tell you how much they charge for copying, printing, and paralegal services, strike those out and give them your outside counsel guidelines instead. The outside counsel guidelines are the business owner's best weapon against overbearing lawyers and overreaching engagement letters. A copy of these guidelines can be found below under the heading "Outside Counsel Guidance and Procedures."

4. Require the attorney to scan documents rather than printing and copying and then charge you for that printing and copying.

5. Prohibit the lawyer from allowing lawyers to do anything a paralegal can do and paralegals from doing anything a secretary can do.

6. Prohibit the lawyer from marking up anything that should be delivered to you at a cost, such as third-party services.

7. Require budgets and that any changes to budgets have prior written approval from you before going over budget.

Leverage

Remember, if you absolutely need to hire a specialist from a large firm in a big downtown office for a small case that will generate around $15,000 in fees, don't expect them to take your outside counsel guidelines seriously. Leverage plays a crucial role in legal fee negotiations, just as it does in any contract negotiation.

Outside Counsel Guidance and Procedures

The following is a sample template to use when hiring outside counsel.

Your firm has been selected to represent _____ in connection with one or more legal matters. We look forward to working with you. The purpose of this letter is to establish our mutual understanding and agreement as to our expectations with respect to your firm's representation of our company.

The scope of your engagement, your billable rate, and other case- or matter-specific information should be set forth by separate cover. However, to the extent that an engagement letter or agreement has been executed previously, contemporaneously with, or subsequent to your receipt and execution of this letter, the terms of this letter shall govern in the event of any inconsistency or ambiguity between them.

Communication. Open and concise communication is essential between your firm and us. We will be actively involved in the case, directing strategy, locating in-house and industry-wide experts, evaluating settlement opportunities, monitoring the case, and providing support. Please send us copies of all correspondence, memoranda, notes, and research (only where either is important and not incorporated into a memo), and briefs and pleadings. No motion should be made or agreed upon with another party without our prior approval. In general, we will review all briefs and pleadings before they are filed; therefore, draft briefs and pleadings should be submitted in ample time to allow for review and input. Prior to commencing discovery, such as interrogatories or depositions, prior approval is required. Prior approval is also required for legal research and memoranda, which are expected to take longer than two hours to complete.

We request a written acknowledgment within one business day following receipt of an assignment. For all litigation, after you have completed your initial review, please provide us with your proposed litigation plan and budget (the "Litigation Plan") at your earliest convenience within five days after a matter has been assigned to your firm. An outline of topics to be included in this Litigation Plan is attached. We expect the Litigation Plan to be updated as the facts and circumstances may require 60 days prior to trial, at the close of discovery, or upon scheduling of mediation, whichever is earlier. For example, if you conclude that your initial budget is understated, please send a revised budget immediately. Since the Litigation Plan will benefit both [insert client name] and your firm, time spent in preparing it should not be charged to us. Actual billings will be tracked against cost estimates set forth in the Litigation Plan. Overruns in excess of ten percent (10%) will not be paid unless we review and approve the circumstances that cause the overrun. For all non-litigation matters, please provide us with a general plan of action and a proposed budget, along with periodic updates on a monthly basis.

Staffing. Different cases obviously require different degrees of expertise. We expect that appropriate staff will be assigned to the matter at the outset so as to handle it expeditiously and on an efficient and cost-effective basis. Along with your initial assessment, please submit for review and approval all attorneys and support staff, including their specific areas of responsibility, qualifications, and billing rate. Once the staff is set, changes should be few. Additional lawyers, consultants, or experts may not be retained without prior approval.

We retained your firm because of your expertise. Accordingly, time spent educating lawyers within the law firm on applicable substantive law should not be billed to us. We will not pay for fees associated with the training of attorneys, including time spent by attorneys as a learning experience or with a transfer of attorneys during an engagement, nor will we pay (and we expect not to be billed) for legal research needed to educate attorneys in basic fields of expertise on the basis of which the firm was chosen.

Generally, we will only pay for one timekeeper for in-firm conferences or duplicated entries for redoing the work of another or reviewing and analyzing documentation and legal research. Discussions or conferences between or among attorneys that result in multiple billing entries should be minimized or avoided. They should only be undertaken when that is the most efficient means possible to convey or obtain information. Billing descriptions for such conferences should indicate why a conference was needed (an entry "Conference with MJK re status" is not sufficient). Where more than one attorney or paraprofessional is involved in the same work project—such as writing a brief or attending a meeting or deposition—the details in the billing statement should make clear why the other person or persons' presence was necessary. Also, please do not duplicate research previously done and take maximum advantage of models and appropriate documents from similar matters. If there is a need for more than one attorney to attend depositions, hearings, trials, or similar matters, call me to discuss the need and obtain approval. If approval is not obtained, we reserve the right to decline to pay at any time other than that of the most senior attorney.

We require that only professional (attorney and paralegal) services be billed. Additionally, paralegal-type work performed by attorneys will be paid at the paralegal rate. Functions that we consider are best performed by a paralegal will only be paid for at the paralegal rate. Non-professional services, which we consider to be firm overhead and for which we should not be billed, including without limitation: secretarial time; typing; time spent proofreading/revising documents (other than substantive revisions); scheduling meetings and appointments; calendaring; conflicts checks; cover letters; preparation of Notices of Deposition; organization and indexing of files, binders, and notebooks (if it does not require professional judgment); bates/date stamping, pick-up and delivery of documents; telephone calls and correspondence to copy services, court reporters, record clerks, court personnel; copying and binding; filing; inventory of documents; opening/closing files; travel arrangements; preparing invoices and responding to billing questions. Paralegal functions include, without limitation: preparation of subpoenas; organizing files in response to production requests; indexing files (if a professional judgment is required); preparation of routine correspondence and pleadings such as demand letters (in simple matter); petition (in simple matter); answers; substitutions of attorney; interrogatories (standard or form); requests to produce (standard or form); Rule 11-type agreements; jury trial demands; motions to compel (standard or form); summarization of records and answers to interrogatories; standard releases; standard orders and standard stipulations. We understand that many paralegal functions may require review by an attorney. We do not pay for overtime or for travel time.

Invoices. Please forward your invoices for services rendered and costs expended on a monthly basis or whenever the total bill (fees and expenses) exceeds $5000, whichever occurs first. All invoices must be itemized by matter, and each matter must include a cumulative total for services and expenses (services and expenses totaled separately) since you began representing us in the matter and since [insert date, e.g., January 1] of the current year. The invoices should include the names and billing rates of all attorneys and others whose time is included on the invoice. You should attach to, or make part of, all bills a printout of time and charges, which shall list for each time entry the identity of the timekeeper, a full description of activities performed, the amount of time spent, the date the services were performed, the individual billing rates, and the total costs. All entries will be billed in tenths of an hour increments.

All entries should be as detailed as possible (no "Attention to..."). Block billing is unacceptable. For example, if numerous tasks are undertaken in one day, they should each be identified with a specific time for performing that task. We will also closely scrutinize any single time-keeper's entry that covers more than eight hours of time in a single day. We will not pay for leaving messages or voicemails nor for listening to them.

Expenses should be itemized separately. A paid receipt must accompany any disbursement item exceeding

$500. If a charge is paid, which upon review should not have been paid, we retain the right to obtain reimbursement. We reserve the right to audit all bills and files using either in-house auditors or the services of an independent auditor. We reserve the right to require additional information with your invoice and/or that you reorganize the information currently requested. We do not pay charges for the time spent preparing bills, reviewing, or discussing them. Invoices for all matters are to be sent to my attention.

Expenses. We expect your firm will use its best efforts to minimize out-of-pocket expenses. All expenses should be billed at actual cost and not include any markup. Exceptional expenses, such as expert witness fees, may be forwarded directly to me for processing along with a signed W-9. Any individual expense expected to exceed $500 must be pre-approved. General overhead and administrative costs are considered part of the hourly rate. Therefore, we will not pay for such costs, including but not limited to word processing time, postage, local meals, entertainment expenses, local transportation and parking fees, review and preparation of firm invoices, charges for use of in-house conference rooms, heating and air conditioning costs and computer research. Photocopy charges may not exceed 3 cents per copy. There shall be no charges for faxes or long-distance calls other than actual, outgoing long-distance charges.

All travel must be pre-approved. All rental cars are to be mid-sized only. Air travel will be coach fare. Although attorneys may request approval for hired cars and business-class airfare for international air travel, approval will be case- and fee-dependent. Hotel and meal rates should be reasonable, and neither personal/incidental expenses nor lavish meals will be reimbursed.

Please sign and return a copy of this letter to indicate your agreement to the terms set forth herein. Please also send me a completed W-9 so our accounting department may set you up as a vendor. If you have any questions, please do not hesitate to call me at

_____.

We look forward to working with you and to a mutually beneficial and enduring relationship.

Sincerely,

Read and Agreed to:
Firm: _____
By: _____
Dated: _____

Disclaimer

The following sample templates and checklists are provided for informational purposes only. Like the rest of the information in this book, they are not intended to establish an attorney-client relationship or serve as legal advice. The use of these templates and checklists does not substitute for the need for consultation with a qualified attorney.

These templates are offered as a general resource to provide a starting point for understanding the processes and subject matter contained therein. However, each situation is unique, and the specific facts and circumstances of your case and your business will require individualized legal analysis.

We therefore strongly recommend that you consult with a licensed attorney to review and customize these templates and checklists to meet your specific needs. Your attorney can provide guidance tailored to your particular situation and ensure that the resulting documents and policies comply with applicable laws and regulations.

By accessing and using these templates and checklists, you acknowledge that it is not a substitute for professional legal advice and that you will seek the assistance of a qualified attorney before implementing or relying on any provisions contained within it. The use of the templates and checklists without the guidance of an attorney is done at your own risk, and no liability shall be attributed to their creators or distributors for any consequences arising therefrom.

Appendix A: Alternative Dispute Resolution (ADR) Clause Template

Dispute Resolution Template

1. Notice; Cure; Negotiations

In the event of any dispute, controversy, or claim arising out of or related to this Agreement or any breach or termination of this Agreement and the Services provided under the Agreement, excluding [EXCLUDED DISPUTES, examples include nonpayment of fees, matters that can be brought in small claims court, breach of confidentiality, breach of intellectual property rights], but including any other alleged violation of any federal, state, or local statute, regulation, common law, or public policy, whether sounding in contract, tort, or statute (the "Dispute"), the Party asserting the Dispute shall send written notice of the Dispute (the "Dispute Notice") to the other Party (the "Notified Party") that includes a written description of the facts and issues of the Dispute. The Notified Party may cure the alleged breach or circumstances underlying the Dispute for thirty (30) calendar days following its receipt of the Dispute Notice. If the Notified Party fails or refuses to cure the alleged breach or circumstances underlying the Dispute within the thirty- (30-) day cure period, then the Parties shall, within five (5) business days following the expiration of the thirty- (30-) day cure period, engage in face-to-face negotiations in an attempt to resolve the Dispute.

2. Mediation

Within sixty (60) calendar days following the Parties' failure to achieve a negotiated resolution to the Dispute, the Parties shall choose a mutually agreeable third-party neutral to mediate the Dispute between the Parties. Mediation shall be non-binding and confidential. The Parties shall refrain from court action and/or arbitration proceedings with respect to any Dispute during the mediation process insofar as they can do so without prejudicing their legal rights. The Parties shall participate in good faith in accordance with the recommendations of the mediator and shall follow the procedures for mediation as suggested by the mediator. The Parties shall share equally all expenses of the mediation, except for the expenses of the individual Parties. Each Party shall be represented in the mediation by a person with authority to settle the Dispute.

3. Arbitration

If the Parties are unable to resolve the Dispute within thirty (30) calendar days of initiating mediation pursuant to Section 1(b), each Party agrees to submit any and all Disputes to the American Arbitration Association ("AAA") for binding arbitration. The Parties shall hold the arbitration in Cleveland, Ohio, USA, before a single arbitrator in accordance with the AAA Commercial Rules of dispute resolution, which are available here at adr.org/rules.

Any arbitral award determination shall be final and binding upon the Parties. Judgment on the arbitrator's award may be entered in any court of competent jurisdiction. THE ARBITRATION SHALL PROCEED ONLY ON AN INDIVIDUAL BASIS. THE PARTIES WAIVE ALL RIGHTS TO HAVE THEIR DISPUTES HEARD OR DECIDED BY A JURY OR IN A COURT TRIAL AND THE RIGHT TO PURSUE ANY CLASS OR COLLECTIVE CLAIMS

AGAINST EACH OTHER IN COURT, ARBI-
TRATION, OR ANY OTHER PROCEEDING.
Each Party shall only submit its individual
claims against the other and will not seek to
represent the interest of any other person. The
arbitrator shall have no jurisdiction or authority to compel any class or collective claim or to
consolidate different arbitration proceedings
with or join any other Party to an arbitration
between the Parties.

Appendix B: Must-Have Clauses in Your Customer Contracts

In Chapter 1, we discussed the importance of engaging with your customers using an attorney-drafted customer contract and highlighted a few of the important clauses to include in that contract. Here, we are going to take a deeper dive into the contract clauses that we view as a must-have in your customer agreements. Please use this as a checklist when evaluating your existing customer contracts and any drafted contracts you receive from your attorney.

Broadly speaking, your business does one of two activities: manufacturing and selling goods or providing and selling services. The legal landscape for sales of goods and sales of services is distinct and different, which means that your customer agreements need to be tailored to the kind of business you have. What if you provide both goods and services? Then you need to analyze the goods and services purchased by your customer to determine whether the engagement is primarily for goods or services. A good short-hand way to analyze this is to determine whether the goods or services account for most of the total cost. Often, the component that constitutes a higher dollar amount of the total customer purchase is considered primary.

For contracts that are primarily services, use a service agreement. For those primarily for the sale of goods, use an agreement tailored for the sale of goods. The classic example of a customer engagement that includes both goods and services is the sale of a piece of equipment with a commitment to provide training on how to use the equipment. Here, the training services are merely incidental to the equipment (the thing the customer wants is the equipment) and likely will be lower cost than the equipment price. This is primarily a deal for goods, so you should use a contract for the sale of goods.

Contracts for the Sale of Goods Between Merchants

There are broadly three kinds of customers to which you can sell goods:

- Merchants: Persons or entities that buy and sell goods or services for a profit
- Non-merchant businesses: Entities that buy goods primarily for personal use and not for resale or commercial purposes
- Consumers: Individuals or entities who purchase goods or services for personal or household use and not for resale or commercial purposes

Contracts for the sale of goods between merchants are very often the result of communications between purchasing departments and key employees of the buyer and seller merchants, typically with attachments (like purchase orders, sales orders, quotes, etc.) capturing the business terms of the deal, namely price and quantity.

The result is typically a myriad of papers and communications that form the basis of the contract. The attachments that get circulated between the parties will sometimes have terms and conditions attached to them that each side hopes will make it into the contract. If these contracts are litigated, one of your litigator's first tasks is to analyze the various communications and forms sent between the parties to determine what the contract is, or at least should be, from your position. The other side's lawyer will often take a different position. This argument is called the battle of the forms and is based on the Uniform Commercial Codes' allowance for business owners to make contracts without strict formality.

While informality helps grease the path to a deal at the beginning, it can create litigation issues that must be expensively argued. With our suggested contract terms below, the contract will contain good protection for your business with terms that will increase the chance that your desired terms will be included in the contract, thus strengthening your litigation position and, ideally, a quicker and easier settlement.

Must-Have Clauses in Sale of Goods Contracts

1. Goods

a. A description of the goods purchased.

b. Quantity of the goods purchased.

c. Price of the goods.

d. Specifications for conforming goods, if any.

2. Contract-Formation Clauses

a. A statement that your acceptance of the contract is conditioned on the customer's agreement to your terms and conditions.

b. A statement that any form of customer agreement that contains additional or different terms is rejected and not included in the agreement between the parties.

c. That acceptance of the goods purchased constitutes acceptance of your terms and conditions and that those terms and conditions form the entire agreement between the parties.

d. That no course of dealings between the parties' supplements or explains any of the terms and conditions.

3. Termination

a. You have the right to begin production or ship goods in stock immediately.

b. Customer cannot terminate without your written consent.

c. Charges will apply for cancellation for all work performed.

4. Shipment and Delivery

a. Manner of Shipment: FOB, CIF, and other

b. Location of Shipment

c. Risk of Loss: Risk of loss shifts to the customer when the goods are put into possession of a common carrier.

d. Delivery Date:

 i. As soon as practicable.

 ii. All delivery dates are your best estimates and approximates based on the availability of materials, labor, etc.

 iii. *Force majeure* language excusing delivery for acts of God or government.

5. **Price**

   a. Subject to change based on:

      i. Alterations to the order, the goods, the specifications, etc.

      ii. Cost of fuel, material, labor, and other

      iii. New legislation, including tax legislation

   b. No discounts unless in writing on the purchase order.

   c. Prices do not include federal, state, or local taxes, and they will be added to the sales price when the seller is obligated to collect them.

   d. Obligation for the customer to reimburse you for taxes paid.

6. **Payment**

   a. Timing of payment (e.g., net thirty from the date of invoice)

   b. Ability to terminate or refuse to perform under the agreement if the customer fails to pay any amounts when due

   c. Non-liability for non-performance which arose from the customer's non-payment

d. Ability to charge interest on delinquent payments

e. Recovery of fees or expenses incurred in attempting to collect the unpaid amounts or for any legal action to recover

f. Additional security for any amounts due and obtain a security interest in the goods purchased

7. Returns

a. Impose requirements for returning goods:

   i. Email notification

   ii. Goods to be packaged for return

   iii. Proof of purchase (invoice) included

   iv. Shipped to a specified address

   v. Goods returned are in a new and unused condition

   vi. Returns are subject to your inspection

   vii. Refunds issued only after receipt of goods in compliance with these requirements

   viii. Restocking charge (offset against any amounts owed to the customer)

     ix. Credit paid after a satisfactory inspection by you (at your sole discretion)

     x. No credit for returned goods lost or damaged in shipment to you

     xi. Customer pays all shipping charges for the return

   b. Timing for payment of credit for compliant returns

8. **Warranty**

   a. Include your business's standard warranty.

   b. Warranty becomes void if anyone other than you repairs the purchased goods.

9. **Disclaimer:** Include a statement that, except for the express warranty, the goods are provided "as is" and that you disclaim all warranties express and implied, including the following warranties, which must be explicitly identified:

   a. Implied warranty of merchantability

   b. Implied warranty of fitness for a particular purpose

10. Exclusive Remedy

    a. If any goods are defective, the customer's sole and exclusive remedy is the replacement or repair of the goods.

    b. Availability of this remedy is subject to your inspection of the allegedly defective goods and determination that the defect is not the result of the customer's misuse of the goods.

11. Limitation of Liability

    a. Limit liability to repair or replace the goods or, if you so elect, a refund of the amount paid for the defective goods.

    b. State that the customer is not entitled to recover incidental or consequential damages.

12. Technical Advice

    a. Any technical advice provided to the customer respecting the goods is without charge, and you assume no obligation or liability for the advice given.

    b. Customers accept it at their own risk.

13. **Indemnification:** The customer should indemnify you against third-party claims arising from the customer's misuse of the goods or any IP infringement resulting from manufacturing the goods in ac-

cordance with the customer's specifications or the customer's combination of the purchased goods with other goods.

14. **Intellectual Property:** You retain all intellectual property rights in the purchased goods.

15. **Confidentiality:** The customer shall treat the goods and all information provided to the customer by you to be confidential and refrain from disclosure of that information.

16. **Collection Fees:** Include a clause that entitles you to pursue collection fees if you need to start a collection action against the customer.

17. **Notices:** Specify where and how to send notices to each party.

18. **Severability:** State that unenforceable clauses do not affect the other obligations under the contract.

19. **Amendments:** Require that all amendments to the contract be in writing and signed by you and the customer.

20. **Waiver:** Include a section clarifying that past waivers do not prevent future demands for strict performance with the services agreement.

21. **Assignment**

   a. Prevent the customer from assigning the agreement without your written approval.

   b. You should be able to freely assign the services agreement.

22. **Alternative Dispute Resolution:** Include a tailored version of the ADR (Alternative Dispute Resolutions) clause included in Appendix A. If you are in an industry in which enforcement of an arbitration clause requires a separate agreement, create a separate ADR agreement to attach to the services agreement.

23. **Choice of Law:** Require the law of your home jurisdiction.

24. **Choice of Forum:** Require lawsuits to be brought in your home state, in your home city/county, or if the customer rejects your home forum, choose a neutral state and county.

25. **Equal Opportunity Employer:** Require you and the customer to comply with the Equal Opportunity clause, Section 202 of Executive Order 11246, as amended, relative to equal employment opportunities and implementing rules and regulations of the Secretary of Labor.

Must-Have Clauses in Customer-Facing Services Agreements

1. Defining the Commitment

    a. Services: Clear definition of the services to be provided

    b. Standard of Acceptance: Objective standard for evaluating when the services are completed and must be accepted by the customer

2. Payment

    a. Fees: Fees for performing the services and the basis on which the fees will accrue (e.g., hourly, completion of a milestone, flat fee for the whole engagement)

    b. Expenses: Allowance for changing additional reasonable expenses to the customer

    c. Taxes: Imposes the obligation for paying taxes related to the services on the customer

    d. Manner of Payment (describe the following):

        i. How the customer must pay you (e.g., wire transfer, check, ACH)

ii. When the payment must be made (e.g., before or after performing the services, after receiving an invoice)

iii. The frequency of payment (e.g., monthly, one-time payment, after milestone completion)

e. Invoices: If you are sending an invoice for the service fees and expenses, describe what will be included and the frequency of delivering the invoice.

f. Late Payment: Describe what happens if the customer fails to pay on time. Items to include:

i. Delinquent payment fee or accruing interest on past due payments

ii. The right for you to suspend services until the customer becomes current

g. Modification: The right for you to increase or decrease the fees with written notice to the customer

3. **Warranties and Disclaimers**

a. Warranty: Include a warranty that you are comfortable with providing based on your business and service level capabilities. Typically, we see warranties only that the services will be performed professionally and in accordance with industry standards and the standards and specifications included in the agreement.

b. Disclaimer: Disclaim all other warranties, express and implied.

c. Exclusive Remedy:

    i. Require the customer to send notice of any breach of warranty.

    ii. Allow for you to cure the breach of warranty for a reasonable period after receiving the notice.

    iii. Limit the customer's remedy for breach of warranty to a refund of the fees already paid, minus any fees for services received or used by the customer.

d. Limitation of Liability: Include a section limiting your damages to only compensatory damages.

e. Liability Cap: Specify that your aggregate liability shall not exceed a certain reasonable amount.

4. **Indemnification:** Require the customer to indemnify you for breach of the services agreement and misuse of the services.

5. **Compliance with Law:** Require that you and the customer comply with applicable law in the per-

formance of each party's obligations under the services agreement.

6. **Collection Fees:** Include a clause that entitles you to pursue collection fees if you need to start a collection action against the customer.

7. **Notices:** Specify where and how to send notices to each party.

8. **Severability:** State that unenforceable clauses do not affect the other obligations under the contract.

9. **Amendments:** Require that all amendments to the contract be in writing and signed by you and the customer.

10. **Waiver:** Include a section clarifying that past waivers do not prevent future demands for strict performance with the services agreement.

11. **Assignment**

   a. Prevent the customer from assigning the agreement without your written approval.

   b. You should be able to freely assign the services agreement.

12. **Relationship of the Parties**

   a. State that the relationship is between independent contractors.

b. You control the manner and method of performing the services.

c. The customer only inspects, evaluates, and expresses satisfaction with the results of the services.

d. The customer has no right to supervise, control, or direct the details and manner of performing the services.

e. The contract shall not be construed as creating an agency, partnership, joint venture, employment, or fiduciary relationship between you and the customer.

f. Neither party can bind the other party.

13. **Alternative Dispute Resolution:** Include a tailored version of the ADR clause included in Appendix A. If you are in an industry in which enforcement of an arbitration clause requires a separate agreement, create a separate ADR agreement to attach to the services agreement.

14. **Choice of Law:** Require the law of your home jurisdiction.

15. **Choice of Forum:** Require lawsuits to be brought in your home state, in your home city/county, or if the customer rejects your home forum, choose a neutral state and county.

16. *Force Majeure*: Excuse performance in the event of an act of God (excluding payment for services already performed).

Appendix C: How to Reduce the Risk of Premises Liability Claims

In Chapter 1, we briefly detailed what premises liability is and the steps that you can take to reduce your risk of premises liability claims. In this appendix, we will provide you with a step-by-step process that, if followed, will reduce the risk of customers being injured at your location and, if an injury occurs, reduce the risk that you will be held liable. The best method for reducing your risk of litigation is by taking measures to prevent injuries from happening, which is the core of this process.

Process for Reducing the Risk of Customer Injury

1. **Understand Premises Liability.** Take the time to learn the law of premises liability by reading this book and consulting with your attorney on premises liability in your state.

2. **Injury Response Procedure.** With your attorney and employees, create an injury response plan de-

tailing how employees should respond to customer injuries. Critical actions to include in the plan are taking pictures of the incident area immediately after the incident, saving any records and paperwork associated with the incident, interviewing the customer and employees to gather information on the incident, using signage cautioning customers of the hazard while gathering information and, after quickly obtaining pictures of the scene, removing the hazard that allegedly caused the injury to prevent further injuries.

3. **Buy General Liability Insurance**. Obtain general liability insurance that protects your business from damages for bodily injury and property damage based on premises liability. Review the exclusions with your attorney to ensure that the policy does not exclude premises liability claims.

4. **Conduct a Risk Assessment**.

    a. Review past injury incidents and perform a root cause analysis with your team, including any personnel who work in the areas where the injury occurred, to determine the root cause of the incident. We recommend using the Ishikawa diagram[1] to sketch out the possible causes.

    b. Walk the floor of your location and identify potential hazards that can harm customers. This will help to capture potential modes of injury that have not happened yet but may happen in the future. We recommend using a failure mode effect analysis to catalog the injury modes, assign a risk to each injury mode, prioritize the injury modes by risk, and identify corrective measures. This is an invaluable tool for reducing or eliminating risks and failures in your business beyond premises liability.

c. Use root cause analysis to determine the root causes of the injury modes identified in step 4(b).

5. **Create and Implement Corrective Measures**.

a. Brainstorm potential corrective measures with your team to resolve, eliminate, or reduce the likelihood or severity of the root causes and injury modes identified in step 2.

b. Analyze each corrective measure based on its potential impact on improving the root cause and cost-effectiveness.

c. Implement the corrective measures that yield the highest impact with a low to moderate cost.

Create standard operating procedures for the implemented corrective measures.

Train your employees in the standard operating procedures.

Make compliance with the standard operating procedures a part of the employee's performance review.

1. **Repeat Step 4**. Repeat step 4 in all the following circumstances:

   a. Whenever a customer injury occurs

   b. After the implementation of any corrective measures

   c. Periodically, at least yearly

2. **Repeat Step 5**. If your root causes analyses and brainstorming during steps 4 and 6 reveal further high-impact corrective actions for root causes and injury modes that have a moderately low to high-risk profile, repeat step 5 to implement new, different, or additional corrective measures to reduce the risk of injury. Also, if your previous corrective measures have not sufficiently reduced the risk of injury for any root cause or injury mode, repeat step 5 in that instance as well.

Once you have completed steps 1–3, the activities you need to perform to proactively minimize your exposure related to premises liability are the consistent repetition of steps 4 and 5. By repeatedly identifying injury risks and implementing corrective actions, over time, your business will become safer for customers and from premises liability claims.

Appendix D: Information Security Management Checklist

Every company needs an information security management system and a formal written policy to execute that system.

A formal written policy should accomplish the following objectives:

- Ensure security and confidentiality of customer information
- Protect against anticipated threats or hazards to security or integrity of information
- Protect against unauthorized access to or use of information that could result in substantial harm or inconvenience to a customer

This checklist identifies the necessary steps to staff and develop an information security management system and policy for your business.

1. **Establish a Board or Executive team** responsible for developing, reviewing, and managing the information security system.

2. **Designate an Information Security Officer** appointed by the board or executive team and managed by personnel independent of the daily operations of the company.

3. **Identify dedicated cybersecurity resources** with appropriate job titles and areas of responsibility.

4. **Schedule regular meetings or reports** directed to the board or executive team regarding relevant information on security threats and institutional metrics.

5. **Annually report the following** to the board or executive team:

   a. Overall status of the information security program and compliance thereto

   b. Material matters related to information security, such as risk assessment, risk management and control decisions, service provider evaluation, audit and test results, security events or violations, and recommendations for changes to the program

6. **Regularly revise** management programs to document, track, test, authorize, approve, and perform system and environmental changes.

7. **Identify end-of-life assets** to be removed and replaced according to the appropriate replacement schedule, and maintain an updated hardware and software asset inventory.

8. **Establish a clean desk policy** for all employees to include secure storage of sensitive papers and mobile devices, clearing of desks at the end of each day, locking of file cabinets, and, where possible, integrating a paperless environment.

9. **Secure destruction and disposal** of physical and electronic records of sensitive information.

10. **Perform an annual risk assessment** that includes the following:

    a. Asset identification

    b. Risk identification

    c. Risk assessment and measurement—analysis and measure of the risk for likelihood of occurrence and/or impact upon occurrence

    d. Risk mitigation

    e. Risk monitoring

11. **Schedule regular auditing, testing, and monitoring** of key controls through network penetration testing and scanning.

12. **Establish a training program** for all employees conducted at the time of hire and at least annually.

13. **Develop a vendor management risk program** including the following:

    a. Due diligence process for new vendors

    b. Ongoing monitoring process for existing vendors

    c. Contractual requirements for all vendors

    d. Incident response and notification procedures

    e. Cloud vendors

14. **Obtain Cyber Security Liability Insurance coverage** for information security and incident response.

15. **Maintain an updated Network Diagram** that includes the following:

    a. Locations of servers

    b. Virtual machines

    c. Network connections to the internet

    d. User devices

    e. Devices or servers that provide key network services, such as DNS and DHCP

    f. DMZ areas

    g. Location of stored data

    h. VLANS

    i. Wireless networks

    j. Cloud resources

    k. VPN connections to third-party service providers

    l. Remote access entry points for users and employees

16. **Monitor the firewall** with regularly reviewed firewall rules.

17. **Ensure that data is encrypted** at rest and in transit.

18. **Secure and use an intrusion detection and prevention system** with a designated person or team responsible for reviewing and monitoring event reports.

19. **Obtain malware protection and** deploy it on all servers and workstations.

20. **Ensure malicious code protection** and monitor that it is updated and managed.

21. **Establish policies and processes for applying security patches** that follow industry best practices:

   a. Patch status reports generated and reviewed to validate effectiveness

   b. Use automated systems to identify and patch systems

22. **Conduct vulnerability scans** and determine who performs them, what is the frequency, and what is scanned.

23. **Conduct penetration tests** and determine who performs them and the frequency.

24. **Secure Access controls**

   a. Password configuration and expiration

   b. Screen lock or log out after inactivity periods

   c. Multi-factor authentication

   d. Lockout after incorrect login attempts

   e. Help desk procedures for failed logins

   f. No shared accounts

   g. Access limited to business need/least privilege

    h. Administrative privileges assigned only as needed

    i. Defined remote access procedures

25. **Establish Access review**

    a. Perform quarterly access review audits

    b. Have procedures and checklists for disabling user accounts and access rights for terminated and/or transferred employees

26. **Set standards for company-issued or personal mobile device controls**

    a. Types of data accessed or stored

    b. Patch management processes

    c. Security auditing and monitoring capabilities

    d. Anti-virus and anti-malware

    e. Remote wipe capabilities

    f. Drive encryption

    g. Secure wireless networks/connections or VPN usage.

27. Establish Business Continuity and Disaster Recovery Plans

a. Documented and appropriate for the size and complexity of the organization based on the following considerations:

i. Business impact analysis

ii. Risk Assessment

iii. Pandemic issues

iv. Essential business functions are identified, and associated contingencies are in place

v. Recovery objectives, and restoration priorities are defined

vi. Contingency locations are included for continued operations

vii. Responsibilities and decision-making authorities for designated teams and/or staff members with contact information

viii. Communication procedures are outlined for contacting employees, vendors, regulators, municipal authorities, emergency response personnel, and customers

b. Reviewed at least annually and updated as necessary

    c. Tested at least annually, and results of the test are documented

       i. Testing includes systems and personnel using different methods

       ii. Remediation plans are developed to address identified gaps

       iii. Remediation efforts are tracked and reviewed regularly

28. **Ensure that a data backup** program and system are in place.

    a. Data is backed up regularly and tested.

    b. Data is stored offline and/or off-site to mitigate the risk of ransomware attacks on the online backup.

    c. Information can be successfully restored from backups, and business operations can resume.

29. **Have an Incident Response Plan**

    a. Responsibilities and decision-making authorities are designated for specific teams and/or team members.

   b. Guidelines for notifying customers, law enforcement, vendors, and regulatory agencies of incidents involving unauthorized access to or use of
   sensitive customer information.

      i. Knowledge of reporting requirements enact-
      ed by state and federal laws or regulations
      specific to industry/business

   c. Reviewed, tested, and updated at least annually

30. **Conduct Information System Monitoring** with
   event logs that are collected and stored in a cen-
   tralized location for later review.

Appendix E: Website Accessibility Checklist

In Chapter 1, we discussed the importance of making your website accessible to persons with disabilities and some practices to consider. These practices are required to comply with the Americans with Disabilities Act and can also improve the scope of customers able to interact with your website, brand, and products. Below is a checklist for you to assess the accessibility of your business's website. When using this checklist, you should include your website's developer and potentially your IT personnel or service provider if you have personnel or contractors providing these services. Also, we recommend using online website accessibility and ADA compliance checkers, in addition to your own review, to double-check compliance.

Needed Information and Materials: To assess the accessibility of your website, you will need:

- A copy of your Website Accessibility Policy, if already created

- Information describing specific actions taken to make your existing website accessible to people with disabilities

- Information about website accessibility training taken by staff and/or contractors responsible for developing and posting webpages and content

- Information about any procedures used to obtain input from people with disabilities regarding the accessibility of your website

- Any input provided by people with disabilities about their experiences accessing your website

- The assistance of your website manager

Analyzing your Web Pages and Website Content: Answer the following questions to determine whether your business's website has any of the most frequent accessibility problems:

1. Does the top of each page with navigation links have a "skip navigation" link? (This feature directs screen readers to bypass the row of navigation links and start at the web page content, thus enabling people who use screen readers to avoid having to listen to all the links each time they move to a new page.)

2. Do all links have a text description that can be read by a screen reader (not just a graphic or "click here")?

3. Do all the photographs, maps, graphics, and other images on the website currently have HTML tags (such as an "alt" tag or a long description tag) with text equivalents of the material being visually conveyed?

4. Are all the documents posted on your website available in HTML or another text-based format (for example, rich text format [RTF] or word processing format), even if you are also providing them in another format, such as Portable Document Format (PDF)?

5. If your website has online forms, do HTML tags describe all the controls (including all text fields, checkboxes, drop-down lists, and buttons) that people can use to complete and submit the forms?

6. If your website has online forms, does the default setting in drop-down lists describe the information being requested instead of displaying a response option (e.g., "your age" instead of "18–21")?

7. If a web page has data charts or tables, is HTML used to associate all data cells with column and row identifiers?

8. Do all video files on your website have audio descriptions of what is being displayed to provide access to visually conveyed information for people who are blind or have low vision?

9. Do all video files on your website have written captions of spoken communication synchronized with the action to provide access to people who are deaf or hard of hearing?

10. Do all audio files on your website have written captions of spoken communication synchronized with the action to provide access to people who are deaf or hard of hearing?

11. Have all web pages been designed so they can be viewed using visitors' web browser and operating system settings for color and font?

Policies and Procedures

Answer the following questions to identify issues in your ongoing procedures to achieve and maintain website accessibility.

1. Do you have a written policy on website accessibility?

2. Is the website accessibility policy posted on your website in a place where it can be easily located?

3. Have procedures been developed to ensure that content is not added to your website until it has been made accessible?

4. Does the website manager check the HTML of all new web pages to confirm accessibility before the pages are posted?

5. When documents are added to your website in PDF format, are text-based versions of the documents (e.g., HTML, RTF, or word processing format) added at the same time as the PDF versions?

6. Have in-house staff and contractors received information about the website accessibility policy and procedures to ensure website accessibility?

7. Have in-house and contractor staff received appropriate training on how to ensure the accessibility of your website?

8. Have in-house and contractor staff who create web content or post it on your website received copies of the Department of Justice's technical assistance document "Accessibility of State and Local Government Websites to People with Disabilities"?

9. If your website contains inaccessible content, is a written plan including timeframes in place now to make all your existing web content accessible?

10. Have you posted on your website a plan to improve website accessibility and invited suggestions for improvements?

11. Does your website home page include easily locatable information, including a telephone number and email address, for use in reporting website accessibility problems and requesting accessible services and information?

12. Do you have procedures in place to ensure a quick response to website visitors with disabilities who are having difficulty accessing information or services available via the website?

13. Have you asked disability groups representing people with a wide variety of disabilities to provide feedback on your website's accessibility? (Note: Feedback from people who use a variety of assistive technologies is helpful in ensuring website accessibility.)

14. Have you tested your website using one of the products available on the internet to test website accessibility? (Note: Products available for testing website accessibility include no-cost and low-cost options. These products may not identify all accessibility issues and may flag issues that are not accessibility problems. They are, nonetheless, a helpful tool in improving website accessibility.)

15. Are there alternative ways of accessing web-based information, programs, activities, and services available for people with disabilities who cannot use computers?

If the answer to any of the above questions is "No," then your website may have accessibility issues. You should consult with your website manager and attorney to determine what corrective actions need to be taken to improve your website's accessibility.

Appendix F: Must-Have Clauses in Your Vendor Contracts

In Chapter 2, we discussed the critical need to have a favorable, attorney-drafted vendor agreement for dealing with your suppliers. There, we discussed some of the important clauses and considerations when reviewing your vendor contracts for your engagements for the procurement of goods, as well as engaging a provider for services.

Here, we are going to take a deeper dive into the contract clauses that we view as a must-have in your vendor agreements. Please use this as a checklist when evaluating your existing customer contracts and any drafted contracts you receive from your attorney.

When engaging with vendors, you will be primarily seeking to obtain either goods for your business, such as raw materials for your manufacturing operation or supplies for your offices, or services, such as support for your client service activities or internal business operations.

For contracts that are primarily for the purchase of goods, use an agreement tailored for the sale of goods, which are usually in the form of terms and conditions attached to your purchase order or order acknowledgment forms (or equivalent forms used in your business). For contracts that are primarily for the purchase of services, you will use a services agreement tailored to those services, which can also be referred to as an independent contractor agreement.

For many businesses, there are instances where you will be the buyer and others where you will be the seller. You do not want to use the same standard terms and conditions for buying and selling because the unique perspective, as the buyer, changes what you want out of the deal and the protections that you need to minimize risk. Consequently, you need both customer and vendor agreements to fully protect your business from the risks associated with doing business.

Contracts for the Purchase of Goods Between Merchants

There are broadly three kinds of customers with whom you can sell goods: merchants, non-merchant businesses, and consumers. A merchant is a person who regularly deals with the goods being sold. For example, the manufacturer of goods and the customer-business who purchases those goods in the ordinary course of business are merchants.

Contracts for the purchase of goods between merchants are often the result of communications between purchasing departments and key employees of the buyer and sell-er merchants, typically with attachments (like purchase orders, sales orders, quotes, etc.) capturing the business terms of the deal, namely price and quantity. The result is typically a myriad of papers and communications that form the basis of the contract.

The attachments that circulate between the parties will sometimes have terms and conditions attached to them that each side hopes will make it into the contract. If these contracts are litigated, one of the first tasks of your litigator is to analyze the various communications and forms sent between the parties to determine what the contract is, or at least should be, from your position.

The other side's lawyer will often take a different position. This argument is called the "battle of the forms" and is based on the Uniform Commercial Code's allowance for business owners to make contracts without strict formality when buying and selling goods. While informality helps grease the path to a deal at the beginning, it can create litigation issues that must be expensively argued.

With our suggested contract terms below, the contract will contain good protections for your business with terms that will increase the chance that your desired terms will be included in the contract, thus strengthening your litigation position and ideally resulting in a quicker and easier set-tlement.

Must-Have Clauses in Sale of Goods Contracts

Goods

1. A description of the goods purchased

    a. Quantity of the goods purchased

    b. Price of the goods

    c. Specifications for conforming goods, if any

2. **Contract-Formation Clauses**

    a. A statement that your acceptance of the contract is conditioned on the customer's agreement to your terms and conditions

    b. A statement that any form of customer agreement that contains additional or different terms is rejected and not included in the agreement between the parties

    c. That acceptance of the goods purchased constitutes acceptance of your terms and conditions and that those terms and conditions form the entire agreement between the parties

    d. That no course of dealings between the parties supplements or explains any of the terms and conditions

3. **Termination:** You have the right to terminate at any time without any additional charge.

4. **Shipment and Delivery**

    a. Manner of Shipment: FOB, CIF, etc.

    b. Location of shipment

    c. Risk of Loss: Risk of loss shifts to you only when the goods arrive at your location

    d. Delivery Date:

        i. Prompt delivery

        ii. Strict adherence to the time stipulated for delivery

        iii. Delivery during your ordinary business hours

5. **Price**

    a. The price for the goods purchased is the price stated on the purchase order.

    b. Seller is required to attach an acknowledged delivery receipt and a copy of the purchase order to all invoices or billing statements before you are required to pay.

c. Only properly invoiced amounts are paid.

d. The seller must issue an official receipt confirming payment.

e. No obligation to pay invoices issued more than 90 days after delivery of the goods.

6. Payment

a. Payment is not acceptance or admission of any liability.

b. You may deduct from monies due to the seller any debts and monies due to you in connection with the order for goods and all liabilities that you have incurred that the seller is liable to bear.

c. Determine the timing of payment (e.g., net thirty from the date of invoice).

7. Seller Warranty

a. Include a full warranty, including the following specific warranties:

    i. Goods will correspond with the order description and any applicable specifications.

    ii. Goods are new unless otherwise stated on the order.

    iii. Goods are of acceptable and merchantable quality.

    iv. Goods are fit for any purposes held out by the seller or made known to the seller by you expressly or by implication, and you are relying on the seller's skill and judgment.

    v. Goods will be properly packaged and secured in a manner to enable them to reach their destination in good condition.

    vi. Goods are free from all liens and encumbrances with a full title guarantee.

    vii. Use of goods will not infringe on the intellectual property rights of any third party.

    viii. The seller will comply with applicable laws and regulations in supplying the goods.

    ix. Any goods or data sent to you will not contain any hidden files, damaging programs, programs to restrict your use or access to any programs or devices, and no harmful code.

b. If maintenance services are involved with the purchase of the goods, include the following warranties:

    i. Maintenance is to be performed in a good and skillful manner, using trained and qualified personnel, and in accordance with industry standards and the description and completion criteria contained in the order.

ii. The services will not give rise to claims for intellectual property infringement or misappropriation.

c. A statement that the warranties are in addition to those implied or required by law.

8. **Manufacturer's Warranty:** Require the seller to assign the manufacturer's warranty for any goods made by a previous manufacturer or seller to you.

9. **Remedies**

a. If the goods are delivered late or breach the warranty, you may:

i. Cancel the order without penalty.

ii. Reject the goods (in whole or in part) and return the goods (or any portion of the goods) to the seller at the seller's expense.

iii. Require the seller to repair or replace the rejected goods or to provide a full refund for the price of the rejected goods, if paid, at your election.

iv. Claim damages for any additional costs incurred by the buyer which are attributable to the seller's failure to deliver the goods on the due date.

b. If the goods do not comply with the order (e.g., insufficient quality, wrong measurement, unfit for purpose), the buyer may, at its election:

  i. Reject the goods (in whole or in part) within a reasonable time after delivery and inspection and obtain replacement equivalent goods elsewhere and make a claim for any additional expense incurred against the seller.

  ii. Obtain a refund.

  iii. Require the seller to repair or replace the goods without charge and in a timely manner.

c. The seller is liable for all costs incurred by the buyer to return rejected goods.

d. Include a statement that acceptance of a part of an order does not require you to accept future shipments of non-conforming goods.

10. **Limitation of Liability:** The buyer is not liable for indirect, consequential, special, or incidental damages.

11. **Indemnification:** The seller indemnifies you for any claims involving the goods, claims for intellectual property infringement based on the supply or

your use of the goods, and any deficiency relating to any taxes.

12. **Confidentiality:** You and the seller shall treat the goods and all information provided to the customer by you to be confidential and refrain from disclosure of that information.

13. **Collection Fees:** Include a clause that entitles you to pursue collection fees if you need to start a collection action against the seller.

14. **Notices:** Specify where and how to send notices to each party.

15. **Severability:** State that unenforceable clauses do not affect the other obligations under the contract.

16. **Amendments:** Require that all amendments to the contract be in writing and signed by you and the customer.

17. **Waiver:** Include a section clarifying that past waivers do not prevent future demands for strict performance with the services agreement.

18. **Assignment**

   a. Prevent the customer from assigning the agreement without your written approval.

   b. You should be able to freely assign the services agreement.

APPENDIX F: MUST-HAVE CLAUSES IN YOUR VENDOR...   183

19. **Alternative Dispute Resolution:** Include a tailored version of the ADR clause included in Appendix A. If you are in an industry in which enforcement of an arbitration clause requires a separate agreement, create a separate ADR agreement to attach to the services agreement.

20. **Choice of Law:** Require the law of your home jurisdiction.

21. **Choice of Forum:** Require lawsuits to be brought in your home state, in your home city/county, or if the customer rejects your home forum, choose a neutral state and county.

22. **Equal Opportunity Employer:** Require you and the customer to comply with the Equal Opportunity clause, Section 202 of Executive Order 11246, as amended, relative to equal employment opportunities and implementing rules and regulations of the Secretary of Labor.

Must-Have Clauses in Vendor Services Agreements

1. Defining the Commitment

a. Services: Clear definition of the services to be provided.

b. Standard of Acceptance: The services are only considered accepted and complete upon your written statement that the services provided are satisfactory, in your sole discretion.

2. Payment

a. Fees: The fees for performing the services and the basis on which the fees will accrue (e.g., hourly, completion of a milestone, flat fee for whole engagement).

b. Expenses: Require prior written approval for any expenses.

c. Taxes: Impose the obligation for paying taxes related to the services on the service provider.

d. Manner of Payment: Describe the following:

   i. The manner of paying the service provider (e.g., wire transfer, check, ACH)

   ii. When you must pay (e.g., before or after performing the services, after receiving an invoice)

   iii. The frequency of payment (e.g., monthly, one-time payment, after milestone completed)

e. Invoices: Require invoices with a detailed description of the services rendered, the time spent, and reasonable supporting documentation.

f. Late Payment: Describe what happens if you fail to pay on time. Items to include:

  i. Require notice from the service provider of the late payment.

  ii. Right to cure any late payment after notice.

g. Fee Modification: Prohibit fee increases during the term of the contract.

3. Records

a. Require the service provider to maintain complete and accurate records related to the provision of the services (time spent, materials used, etc.).

b. Provide yourself the right to inspect the records on request.

4. Warranties and Disclaimers

a. Warranty: The services will be performed in a good and skillful manner, only using qualified, trained, and legally authorized personnel, and in accordance with the highest standards in the service provider's industry.

b. Remedy: You may pursue the following actions in response to the service provider's breach:

   i. Obtain injunctive relief prohibiting the service provider from performing further actions that are inconsistent with the services agreement.

   ii. Failure to satisfactorily perform the services on a timely basis results in you having the right to suspend the services, obtain replacement services, assign one of your agents to evaluate the service provider's work to mitigate the effects of the service provider's breach, and withhold payment of any amounts due to set off the damages caused by service provider's breach.

   iii. If either party is required to seek enforcement of the agreement, the unsuccessful party pays the prevailing party its attorneys' fees and costs.

   iv. Remedies are cumulative with those available at law or in equity.

5. **Indemnification:** Require the service provider to indemnify you for claims arising from the service provider's negligence, willful misconduct, or breach of the services agreement.

6. **Compliance with Law:** Require that you and the customer comply with applicable law in the performance of each party's obligations under the services agreement.

7. **Notices:** Specify where and how to send notices to each party.

8. **Severability:** State that unenforceable clauses do not affect the other obligations under the contract.

9. **Amendments:** Require that all amendments to the contract be in writing and signed by you and the customer.

10. **Waiver:** Include a section clarifying that past waivers do not prevent future demands for strict performance with the services agreement.

11. **Assignment**

    a. Prevent the service provider from assigning the agreement without your written approval.

    b. You should be able to freely assign the services agreement.

12. **Relationship of the Parties**

    a. State that the relationship is between independent contractors.

b. The service provider controls the manner and method of performing the services.

c. You only inspect, evaluate, and express satisfaction with the results of the services.

d. Customer has no right to supervise, control, or direct the details and manner of performing the services.

e. Contract shall not be construed as creating an agency, partnership, joint venture, employment, or fiduciary relationship between you and the customer.

f. Neither party can bind the other party.

13. **Alternative Dispute Resolution:** Include a tailored version of the ADR clause included in Appendix A. If you are in an industry in which enforcement of an arbitration clause requires a separate agreement, create a separate ADR agreement to attach to the services agreement.

14. **Choice of Law:** Require the law of your home jurisdiction.

15. **Choice of Forum:** Require lawsuits to be brought in your home state, in your home city/county, or if the customer rejects your home forum, choose a neutral state and county.

16. ***Force Majeure***: Excuse performance in the event of an act of God (excluding payment for services already performed).

Appendix G: Choice of Entity

The decision to start a new business involves numerous important decisions. One of the most critical decisions is determining the correct type of business entity for the venture. This decision affects the operational, management, and decision-making aspects of the business, as well as having profound implications for liability and taxes.

Summary of the Main Business Entity Types

1. **Sole Proprietorship**

   ○ **Definition:** A business directly owned and operated by a single individual.

   ○ **Characteristics**

     • **Control:** The owner maintains complete control and decision-making authority.

     • **Lack of Formalities:** There is no separate and distinct business entity apart from the individual owner; thus, there are nearly no corporate formalities that are necessary to administrate the business.

- **Liability:** The owner is personally liable for all business debts and liabilities.

- **Taxation:** Profits and losses are reported on the owner's personal tax return.

○ **Suitability for Business Owners**

- Generally, not recommended due to unlimited personal liability.

- However, it may be useful for a small business with minimal complexity, no employees, little to no regulatory requirements, and relatively simple customer and vendor relationships.

2. Partnership

○ **Definition:** A business structure owned and managed by two or more individuals, called partners, who share profits, losses, and responsibilities.

○ **Characteristics:** All characteristics depend on the type of partnership formed, as discussed below, but general partnerships formed informally by multiple people have the following characteristics:

- **Shared Control:** The partners share decision-making authority and can each bind the business to obligations, such as contracts.

- **Liability:** The partners are each personally liable for the business's debts and liabilities.

- **Taxation:** Profits and losses are allocated among the partners and reported on the partner's personal tax returns.

○ **Types of Partnerships:** There are numerous different kinds of partnerships that affect the control, decision-making authority, and liability of the partners, such as:

  - **General Partnerships (GP):** All partnerships share control and decision-making authority and are jointly and severally liable for all debts and liabilities of the business.

  - **Limited Partnerships (LP):** Have general partners that control the business and have personal liability and limited partners who enjoy limited liability protection but cannot participate in the day-to-day operation of the business.

  - **Limited Liability Partnership (LLP):** Similar to a general partnership but provides limited liability protection to all partners, similar to a limited liability company. These are often restricted to certain professions or industries depending on the jurisdiction.

- **Limited Liability Limited Partnership (LLLP):** A limited partnership where all partners, including the general partners, have limited liability protections. This is only available in certain states and jurisdictions.

- **Suitability for Business Owners**

  - Partnerships are generally not recommended because of unlimited personal liability for the general partners (for GPs and LPs). Unless your profession or industry is permitted to form as a Limited Liability Partnership, and there is an industry or business-specific reason to avoid forming as a Limited Liability Company, other business entities have attributes that make them better choices for most new businesses.

3. For-Profit Corporations

- **Definition:** A business that is a separate and distinct entity from its owners, called shareholders, which provides limited liability protection.

○ **Characteristics**

- **Limited Liability:** In general, shareholders are not personally liable for the debts and liabilities of the corporation.

- **Taxation:** Corporations are subject to double taxation as a C corporation by default (taxation of profits and dividends). The corporation, if eligible, may elect to be taxed as an S corporation, which subjects the corporation to pass-through taxation, similar to a partnership.

- **Management:** Governed by a board of directors elected by the shareholders.

- **Formalities:** To preserve the legal separateness and limited liability protection, the shareholders and board of directors must regularly undertake certain actions to show that they are treating the corporation as a separate legal entity, such as separating funds of the corporation from the shareholders' personal assets, holding meetings and taking meeting minutes, taking important actions through written resolutions, maintaining a corporate record book, among other actions.

- **Well-Developed Law:** The State of Delaware has a well-developed body of court cases adjudicating disputes between corporations, between shareholders, and between shareholders and the corporation, and that generally favors corporate management. Even if your corporation is not formed in Delaware, it is likely that your jurisdiction will be persuaded by Delaware's decisions.

4. Suitability for Business Owners

- Corporations come with clear upsides, namely, limited liability and well-developed law. However, the formalities and double taxation associated with corporations are turn-offs for business owners who prefer a more flexible structure with fewer formalities. Thus, we generally do not recommend for-profit corporations. If a person already formed a business as a corporation, we recommend either converting to an LLC or adopting a close corporation agreement, if eligible, to simplify the formalities.

5. Limited Liability Company (LLC)

- **Definition:** A business that is a separate and distinct entity from its owners, called members, which provides limited liability protection, a flexible management structure, and partnership taxation.

Characteristics

- **Limited Liability:** In general, members are not personally liable for the debts and liabilities of the company.

- **Taxation:** Limited liability companies are taxed as partnerships by default and thus subject to pass-through taxation. The members will report the company profits allocated to them on their personal tax returns.

- **Management:** May be managed directly by the members or by one or more managers elected by the members. The decision-making processes and control are defined in an operating agreement adopted by the members, which permits the members to craft tailored management and governance of the limited liability company, subject to a few statutory requirements.

- **Formalities:** To preserve the legal separateness and limited liability protection, the members must regularly undertake certain actions to show that they are treating the limited liability company as a separate legal entity, such as separating funds of the corporation from the shareholders' personal assets, taking important actions through written resolutions, maintaining a corporate record book, among other actions. Limited liability company owners typically need to follow fewer formalities compared to corporations.

- **Liberal Law:** Depending on the jurisdiction, the laws affecting limited liability companies generally operate based on freedom of contract (the operating agreement), allowing the business owners more flexibility in how the management of the business works.

- **Suitability for Business Owners**

  - This is the entity type we recommend for most business owners because of its limited liability protection, lack of burdensome formalities, flexibility, and, for some persons, beneficial taxation status.

- **Not-for-Profit Corporation**

  - **Definition:** An organization formed for purposes other than making a profit, often focusing on charitable, religious, or educational activities.

  - **Characteristics**

    - **Mission-Driven:** Operates with the primary goal of furthering a cause.

    - **Tax-Exempt Status:** A not-for-profit corporation may be eligible for 501(c)(3) status, which exempts the organization from certain taxes under certain conditions.

- **No Profit Distribution:** Profits are reinvested into the organization's mission.

○ **Suitability for Business Owners**

- Only suitable for persons looking to create a non-profit venture to forward a charitable, religious, or educational cause.

- **Professional Association**

○ **Definition:** A business association organized for the sole purpose of providing professional services and, if not superseded by the jurisdiction's professional association statute, is generally governed by the jurisdiction's for-profit corporation laws.

○ **Characteristics**

- **Professionals Only:** Only certain professionals may form and take ownership in a professional association. The vocations that are considered to be professional for formation are established by statute.

- **Limited Liability:** Professional associations provide their owners with a degree of limited liability.

- **Corporate Management:** Management and governance are largely similar to a for-profit corporation.

- **Taxation:** Professional associations have a C corporation status by default, which causes double taxation, but like a for-profit corporation, may elect to be an S corporation. Further, professional associations may receive beneficial tax treatment, you should discuss those benefits with your accountant if you are investigating forming your professional service business as a professional association.

- **Suitability for Business Owners**

  - In many cases, professionals can form a standard limited liability company to provide professional services unless the law or professional licensing board in your jurisdiction prohibits it.

  - If there is a legal requirement or tax benefit to forming a professional association, then we recommend forming a professional association. However, forming a conventional limited liability company should also be explored.

See the next Appendix for a flowchart to assist you with selecting a business entity for your new venture.

Appendix H: Choice of Entity Type Flowchart

As discussed in Chapter 3, the type of entity that you form can influence your personal liability for business debts as well as the formalities that you will need to comply with to maintain any limited liability protections associated with that type of entity. If possible, we always recommend that you form a limited liability entity type, such as a corporation or limited liability company, rather than a sole proprietorship or partnership, to protect your personal assets. If you are a professional providing services requiring specific licensure in the state in which you will be engaging in business, such as an attorney, medical doctor, or nurse, you can consider a professional association as well. If you intend to engage in non-profit activities for a social purpose, then you will need to form a non-profit corporation.

For most businesses, the limited liability company will be the best option since it provides limited liability protection with low formalities to comply with compared to the other entity types. Below is a flowchart to assist you in deciding what entity is right for your business or organization.

CHOICE OF ENTITY CHART

Type of Entity	Formation	Liability	Taxation	Upkeep
Sole Proprietorship	No state filings needed. Obtain business permits and trademarks, if applicable.	Business owner is personally responsible for all business debts and obligations.	Pass-through taxation. Owner reports income and expenses on personal income tax returns and is taxed at the individual tax rate.	None.
General Partnership (GP)	Two or more people agree to own a business together. May be outlined in partnership agreement. No state filings needed.	Business owners have shared personal responsible for all business debts and obligations.	Pass-through taxation. Owners report their personal shares of income and expenses on personal income tax returns.	Duration is governed by the Partnership Agreement. There are no management obligations by default.
Limited Partnership (LP)	A formal filing with the state government is required stating the business's purpose and providing the names and general contact information of both limited and general partners.	Business owners are is personally responsible for all business debts.	Pass-through taxation. Owners report their personal shares of income and expenses on personal income tax returns, as laid out in partnership agreement.	Duration is governed by the Partnership Agreement. There are no management obligations by default.
Limited Liability Company (LLC)	A formal filing with the state government is required stating the business's purpose and providing the names and general contact information of statutory agents.	Protects owners from personal liability for acts of the LLC and its members.	Pass-through taxation. Multi-member LLCs must file an informational tax return in addition to reporting personal shares on individual returns.	Consistently maintain state obligations like agent and address requirements.
Professional Partnership	Partners in the same professional industry may form a partnership through a partnership agreement and adherence to their state professional standards. No state filings needed.	Business partners have shared personal responsible for all business debts and obligations.	Pass-through taxation. Partners report their personal shares of income and expenses on personal income tax returns.	Duration is governed by the Partnership Agreement. There are no management obligations by default.
Corporation (C-Corp)	Choose and register an unregistered name, file articles of incorporation in incorporating state, offer stock to shareholders, obtain EIN, establish board of directors.	Offers limited liability protection to owners/shareholders where there is typically no personal responsibility for business debts and obligations.	Corporate income tax imposed on its income, after offsetting income with losses, deductions, and credits.	Must maintain governing bylaws, file annual reports, financial disclosure reports and financial statements. Must hold one annual board meeting, maintaining minutes and voting records.
Non-profit Corporation	Fill out a state application for formation and include a charter and articles of incorporation. If applying for federal tax-exempt status, file 501(c)(3) application.	Offers limited liability protection to directors where there is typically no personal responsibility for business debts and obligations.	Exempt from federal income tax with 501(c)(3) status.	Consistently maintain state obligations like agent and address requirements.

Appendix I: How to Fully Form Your LLC

In Chapter 3, we explained that the formation of your LLC is the first step for starting your new business. Many business owners stop here and never get the full benefit of the new LLC and risk non-compliance with corporate formalities. Whether this is your first business or adding a new venture among your numerous enterprises, please follow this checklist to ensure that your LLC is fully formed.

How to Fully Form Your LLC

1. File the Articles of Organization, Certificate of Formation, or other formation paperwork with the Secretary of State in your intended home state.

   a. This process will require you to appoint a registered agent in the formation state to receive legal process and other correspondence. This agent can be one of the individual members of the LLC, or you can hire a third party to handle the registered agent services for you.

2. Obtain an EIN for the LLC

    a. This is your LLC's tax identification number for tax purposes.

    b. You can obtain this online at: https://www.irs.gov/businesses/small-businesses-self-employed/apply-for-an-employer-identification-number-ein-online

3. Adopt an Operating Agreement

    a. Have an experienced business attorney draft an Operating Agreement for your LLC, specifying the rights and obligations of the members. Please see Appendix Q: Must-Have Clauses in an LLC Operating Agreement (on p. 249).

4. Open a bank account for the LLC

    a. As discussed in Chapter 3, commingling your personal and business assets can put you at risk of losing your LLC's limited liability protections.

    b. Opening a bank account for the LLC and keeping the LLC's cash in that bank account keeps your personal and business funds separate.

5. Business Licenses and Permits

    a. Speak with a business attorney to determine what licenses and permits may be necessary for the operation of your business.

    b. Call your local government office before you start your business to ask about what licenses, permits, and legal requirements apply to the business you intend to start.

6. Taxes

    a. Consult with an accountant on the taxes applicable to your business.

    b. Work with your accountant to set up accounts with the taxation authorities that govern your business for the purpose of paying taxes.

    c. If you intend to do business in multiple states, you will need to engage in this process for every state in which you do business.

7. Recordkeeping

    a. Maintain a binder and electronic file for all of your LLC's corporate records.

    b. At the beginning, your corporate records binder should have the following documents

        i. The certified Articles of Organization (or equivalent filing)

        ii. The EIN notice containing the LLC's EIN and the LLC's Operating Agreement

        iii. Any obtained licenses and permits

      iv. A ledger showing all persons who hold an ownership interest in the LLC

  c. Further, you should establish an electronic and physical document management system for storing other business records, such as contracts, insurance information, past tax returns, financial information, any documents that are required to be maintained under state and federal law, and any other documents that you desire to retain. This system should be easily accessible and navigable to ensure that you can review your LLC's contractual and other obligations from time to time.

8. Operating in Other States

  a. If you intend to operate your business in other states, you must file as a foreign limited liability company in the other states where you intend to do business.

  b. Speak with your accountant about the tax consequences of doing business in those other states.

If you fully form your business in accordance with this checklist, you will have a solid foundation for maintaining legal compliance as you start your new venture.

Appendix J: Must-Have Clauses in an LLC Operating Agreement

In Chapter 3, we mentioned that one of the critical documents you need to ensure proper governance and operation of your business and to manage the relationship between you and your business partners is an Operating Agreement, for LLCs, or a Shareholders Agreement, for corporations. Generally, we recommend forming businesses as LLCs because they provide the most flexibility and ease of administration compared to other entity forms. Please refer to our Choice of Entity Flowchart in Appendix H (see p. 201) for a breakdown of how we view the choice of entity problem.

Because an Operating Agreement is one of the most important documents for the successful operation of your business, we recommend that you have an experienced business attorney draft and tailor it to your needs. However, at a minimum, the Operating Agreement should contain the following must-have clauses to protect you, your business partners, and your business.

Must-Have Clauses in Limited Liability Company Operating Agreements

1. **Formation and Name:** Clearly state the LLC's name, purpose, date of formation, entity number, and duration, if specified.

2. **Members' Contributions:**

   a. Specify each member's initial contribution, whether it be in the form of cash, property, or services.

   b. Identify the rules and processes for future capital contributions, if any, such as the voting threshold for approving future capital contributions.

3. **Allocation of Profits and Losses:** Outline how profits and losses will be allocated among members to ensure fairness.

4. **Distribution of Available Cash:** Establish the process for authorizing and distributing available cash to the members, including whether this is a decision of the members or the manager(s).

5. **Management Structure:**

   a. Indicate whether the day-to-day management of the LLC will be conducted by the members or by one or more managers.

b. Establish in detail the powers and responsibilities of the members, managers, and officers.

c. Include a list of major decisions that cannot be done by any one member or a manager, instead, those decisions will require a member vote.

6. **Meetings and Voting:**

a. Establish rules for meetings and voting to facilitate effective decision-making processes.

b. Include a provision stating that the members and managers can take action without a meeting by unanimous written consent.

7. **Transfer of Membership Interests:**

a. Restrict the members' ability to transfer ownership interests unless approved by the members.

b. Add a right of first refusal to give the LLC and the members the opportunity to buy a fellow member's ownership interest in the face of a third-party offer.

c. Include drag-along and tag-along provisions to promote the member's ability to sell the LLC to third parties.

8. **Withdrawal or Resignation:** Specify the conditions and process for a member to withdraw or resign from the LLC.

9. **Dissolution:** Outline circumstances and procedures for dissolving the LLC and how LLC property should be distributed. This clause should comply with the winding up requirements of your home state.

10. **Buyout and Buy-Sell Provisions:** Include mechanisms for buying out a member's ownership interest in the event of a deadlock or member misconduct.

11. **Non-Compete and Confidentiality:** Specify any restrictions on competitive activities and confidentiality obligations among members.

12. **Taxation:** Discuss the LLC's tax classification and relevant tax provisions for clarity on financial matters. For single-member LLCs, the tax status will be "disregarded entity" by default. For multi-member LLCs, the tax status will be "partnership" by default. Consult with your accountant to determine whether electing to be taxed as an S corporation is beneficial to your business and tax burden.

13. **Indemnification:** Include an indemnification clause that causes the LLC to compensate members, managers, and officers who are sued due to their role as a member, manager, or officer. All indemnification obligations should be subject to member vote on a case-by-case basis.

14. **Succession Planning:**

    a. Address procedures in the event of a member's death or incapacity to ensure a smooth transition.

    b. Specify what happens to a member's ownership interest on the member's death.

        i. Either the LLC or the other members should be given the right to buy back the deceased member's ownership interest from the estate at fair market value, paid to the estate or the beneficiaries in installments over time.

    c. Make sure to clarify that the persons receiving a deceased member's ownership interest will only have the rights of an "assignee" and will not be fully-fledged members of the LLC.

15. **Dispute Resolution:** Include our recommended alternative dispute resolution clause to minimize the risk of ownership disputes.

16. **Amendments to the Operating Agreement:** Outline the process for making changes to the operating agreement as the needs of the LLC evolve. This typically requires a unanimous or supermajority vote of the members.

17. **Governing Law:** Specify the state laws that will govern the LLC to ensure legal clarity.

18. **Members' Schedule:** Attach a schedule show-
ing the names, addresses, ownership interests, and
capital contributions of each member.

Crafting a comprehensive operating agreement using this
checklist will not only protect the interests of all members
but also provide a solid framework for the successful operation of your LLC. Remember, seeking legal advice to
tailor these clauses to your specific situation is always a
wise investment in the long-term success of your business.

Appendix K: Checklist for How to Avoid (or Minimize the Impact of) Partnership Disputes

When the relationship among the owners of a business is positive, proactive, and transparent, the relationship can accelerate the growth of the business. However, when disagreement among the owners concerning the direction of the business is allowed to cause communication to break down and a dispute to arise, the business can grind to a halt. One of the most disruptive disputes that can derail your business is one with your business partners. While not all business owner disputes can be avoided, implementing the recommendations in this checklist can help minimize the impact of partnership disputes and prevent some of them from getting to that point in the first place.

Checklist to Avoid (or Minimize the Impact of) Partnership Disputes

1. Clear Governing Documents

    a. Draft comprehensive governing documents establishing rules on the following issues, which will be described further in subsequent checklist items.

        i. Definition of roles and responsibilities of, and limitations on, the owners

        ii. Indicate the mechanics of call owner meetings

        iii. Specify how decisions are made

        iv. Describe how deadlocks are resolved

        v. Include the waterfall dispute resolution clause provided in Chapter 1, tailored to your governing document

    b. Below is a list of the primary entity types and the relevant documents to adopt.

        i. Corporation

            1. Articles of Incorporation

2. Either a Close Corporation Agreement (for corporations with few shareholders) or Bylaws

ii. Partnership: Partnership Agreement

iii. Limited Liability Company: Operating Agreement

c. See the Must-Have Clause in a Limited Liability Company Operating Agreement in Appendix J for a detailed breakdown of important clauses to include in your business's governing documents.

2. Open Communication

a. Foster open and transparent communication among partners, including scheduling regular meetings with the owners to discuss business operations, goals, potential issues, and other company business, either in person or through video conference.

i. In many cases, your business's governing documents should not require regular meetings of the owners but provide the process for calling, giving notice of, and holding owner meetings.

ii. As a best practice, meetings should be regularly called to discuss salient business issues.

b. If any concerns are raised by an owner, schedule a meeting to address the concerns promptly, brainstorm solutions, and discuss expectations going forward.

3. **Defined Roles and Responsibilities: Limitations**

a. If the individual owners have particular expertise or unique contributions to the business, adopt a written resolution to give the owners individual roles and responsibilities, including limitations on the owner's authority in that role. This will minimize ambiguity in responsibility to prevent misunderstandings among others.

b. Include a list of major decisions that cannot be made by the individual owners and must be approved by the owners with a unanimous or supermajority vote.

4. **Decision-Making Protocols**

a. Write clear protocols for decision-making, especially in situations where there is a high risk of disagreement.

b. Establish the voting thresholds needed to approve major decisions, and any decisions that you decide should be left to the owners.

5. Deadlock

a. Describe in detail how deadlocks are resolved, such as referring the question to a mutually agreeable third party or allowing the disputing owners to buy each other out.

b. Outline the process for buying out a departing partner's share, such as implementing a cross-purchase offer process.

6. Non-Compete and Confidentiality Agreements

a. Implement non-compete and confidentiality agreements to protect the business's interests by clearly outlining restrictions on competing activities and the handling of sensitive information.

7. Transparency

a. Maintain accurate records of the business's finances, business transactions, and operational activities.

b. Require the owners who are actively involved in the business's day-to-day operations to regularly report on the business's financial and operational performance.

c. Regularly share financial statements and updates on the business's financial health to build trust.

8. Insurance Coverage

a. Obtain appropriate insurance coverage, such as liability insurance, to mitigate financial risks.

b. Ensure all partners are aware of the coverage and its implications.

9. Regular Legal Check-ups

a. Periodically review and update legal documents, including the business's governing documents.

b. Ensure ongoing compliance with changing laws and regulations.

10. Succession Planning

a. Plan for the unexpected by establishing a succession plan.

b. Clearly outline the steps to be taken if an owner is unable to continue their involvement in the business.

Appendix L: Checklist for Establishing a Document Management and Retention System

Creating a document management and retention system is crucial for organizations to organize, secure, and appropriately dispose of documents. If a dispute arises, being ready and able to provide your attorney with the information and documents needed to mediate or litigate the dispute quickly is essential for promoting early and efficient resolution of the dispute. Here's a comprehensive checklist to guide the development and implementation of such a system:

Document Management

1. **Inventory**: Create an inventory of all document types and categories within the organization.

2. **Classification**: Establish a standardized system for classifying documents based on type, importance, and sensitivity.

3. **Access Control**: Implement access controls to ensure that only authorized personnel can view, edit, or delete specific documents.

4. **Version Control**: Set up a version control system to track and manage revisions to documents, ensuring that the latest version is always accessible.

5. **Naming Conventions**: Define clear and consistent naming conventions for files to facilitate easy retrieval.

6. **Metadata**: Include relevant metadata (e.g., date created, author, keywords) to enhance search capabilities.

7. **Folder Structure**: Organize documents into a logical folder structure, reflecting the organization's workflow and departments.

8. **Document Lifecycle**: Map out the lifecycle of each document, from creation to archiving or disposal.

Document Retention and Disposal

1. **Retention Policies**: Develop retention policies specifying the duration each type of document should be retained based on legal, regulatory, and business requirements.

2. **Legal Compliance**: Ensure that retention policies comply with relevant local, state, and federal laws and regulations.

3. **Destruction Procedures**: Establish secure procedures for the destruction of documents, whether through shredding, electronic deletion, or other approved methods.

4. **Archiving**: Determine which documents need to be archived for historical or reference purposes and establish a secure archiving process.

5. **Audit Trails**: Implement audit trails to track who accessed, modified, or deleted documents, aiding in compliance and security.

Security Measures

1. **Encryption**: Utilize encryption for sensitive documents to protect them from unauthorized access.

2. **User Authentication**: Implement strong user authentication mechanisms to control access to the document management system.

3. **Backup Procedures**: Regularly back up the document repository to prevent data loss in the event of system failures.

4. **Access Monitoring**: Monitor and log access to the document management system, reviewing logs periodically for suspicious activity.

Training and Awareness

1. **User Training**: Provide comprehensive training to employees on the document management system, including proper usage, classification, and retention practices.

2. **Policy Awareness**: Ensure that all employees are aware of document management and retention policies, emphasizing their role in compliance.

3. **Regular Audits**: Conduct regular audits of the document management system to ensure adherence to policies and identify areas for improvement.

Continuous Improvement

1. **Feedback Mechanism**: Establish a feedback mechanism for users to report issues or suggest improvements to the document management system.

2. **Policy Reviews**: Regularly review and update document management and retention policies with your attorney to adapt to changes in regulations or business practices.

3. **Technology Upgrades**: Stay current with technological advancements and consider upgrades to the document management system to enhance security and functionality.

4. **Benchmarking**: Benchmark the document management system against industry best practices to identify areas for improvement.

5. **Legal Counsel**: Consult legal counsel periodically to ensure ongoing compliance with evolving regulations.

Implementing a robust document management and retention system requires careful planning and ongoing commitment. Regular reviews and updates to the system will ensure that it continues to meet the organization's needs while safeguarding sensitive information and complying with relevant laws and regulations.

Appendix M: Compliance Program Checklist

As we discussed in Chapter 4, there are a myriad of laws and regulations enacted by the federal, state, and local governments that may affect your business. Depending on the size and type of business you are engaged in, the number and scope of laws and regulations with which you will need to maintain compliance is a minefield impossible to navigate on your own. To help you maintain regulatory compliance, we suggest creating a tight working relationship with an attorney familiar with the laws of your industry, as well as hiring or designating dedicated personnel in your business to handle regulatory compliance in accordance with a written compliance program. This checklist identifies the actions that you should take and the legal problems meriting consideration when creating a compliance program.

1. **Identify Compliance Activity.** Identify and review all your company's current compliance activities and the personnel engaged in those activities. This will be the starting point for your future compliance program.

2. **Gain Buy-In.** Identify the key leaders, managers, and employees in your company that will be directly affected by the new compliance program or that are necessary for the creation, development, implementation, or execution of the new compliance program. Hold one-on-one meetings with those personnel to gain buy-in for the new program and gain their assistance with creating, developing, implementing, or executing the compliance program.

3. **Appoint or Hire a Compliance Officer.** Create the position of Chief Compliance Officer for your company and delegate to that person the authority to implement, oversee, and administrate the company's compliance program. This officer has the power and independence to hold other personnel accountable under the compliance program's policies and procedures and access to the governing body of your company (such as the board of directors for a corporation or the manager or members of a limited liability company) to report on and make recommendations with respect to compliance issues. Hire, appoint, or promote a person with past or current high-level management authority and experience in legal compliance. Coordinate all compliance activities and personnel identified in step 1 under a department led by the Chief Compliance Officer. Conduct background checks and screen all individuals assigned or hired to the compliance department under the Chief

Compliance Officer to ensure compliance activities are not being conducted by persons who have violated the law.

4. **Create a Cross-Functional Team to Develop the Compliance Program.** Assemble a team of leaders, managers, and employees in your organization to assist in developing the new compliance program (the **Compliance Program Development Team**). This team will be composed of the Chief Compliance Officer, the key personnel currently engaged in your company's current compliance activities, and other personnel who will be important for implementing and executing the compliance program. Including these internal stakeholders early in the process and providing them a voice in the creation of the new compliance program will create additional buy-in, which will likely result in a quicker and more successful implementation of the compliance program and continued adherence to it post-implementation.

5. **Identify All Applicable Laws and Regulations Affecting Your Business.** Work with the Compliance Program Development Team and your legal counsel to identify all international, federal, state, and local laws and regulations affecting your company.

6. **Create Policies and Procedures to Prevent, Discover, and Remedy Non-Compliance.** Direct your legal counsel and Chief Compliance Officer to prepare policies and procedures to prevent compliance issues, discover non-compliance when it occurs, and remedy any misconduct. Once prepared, the draft policies and procedures should be reviewed by the Compliance Program Development Team to identify any gaps and possible implementation and execution issues. When drafting and reviewing these policies and procedures, you should consider all applicable laws and regulations, common practices in your industry, the size of your company, and past compliance issues and misconduct.

7. **Minimum Policies**. Your compliance program should include, at a minimum, all the following policies and procedures:

   a. Code of Conduct/Ethics

   b. Employment Handbook/Manual

   c. Policies and Procedures for Addressing and Remedying Non-Compliance and Misconduct

8. **Implementation of Compliance Program.** Assign responsibility for and direct the Chief Compliance Officer to implement and oversee the compliance program. Circulate all created policies and

procedures to all employees and require their signed acknowledgment of the policies and procedures.

9. **Access to Programs and Policies.** Work with your information technology department or IT service provider to establish the method for employees to access the compliance program and all policies and procedures electronically.

10. **Training.** Direct the Chief Compliance Officer to train all managers and supervisors on the compliance program and all policies and procedures, including their responsibilities in the execution and administration of the policies and procedures, after the implementation of a new policy and regularly, such as annually. Train all employees in all new policies and procedures at the time of implementation and regularly, such as annually.

11. **Regular Review of the Program.** Schedule regular reviews of your company's compliance program with your legal counsel and Chief Compliance Officer to ensure that the compliance program is updated based on changes to applicable laws and regulations and that it is sufficient to handle any compliance issues that have arisen in the previous year. We recommend reviewing your company's compliance program at least annually.

Appendix N: How to Respond to Government or Regulatory Communications

In Chapter 4, we discussed how government entities or regulatory bodies can impact your business. All companies should have a procedure for handling certain types of communications that can be received from government entities or regulatory bodies, such as complaints, inquiries, requests for information, notices of violation or noncompliance, and so on (collectively, the "Communications"). This checklist sets out a best practices framework for the handling of these communications.

1. **Incoming Correspondence.** Define the department and/or individual(s) within the organization who receive, handle, and process incoming correspondence and ensure they are trained to recognize Communications.

2. **Designate Recipients.** Appoint the department and/or individual(s) to whom the Communications should be delivered and the timeframe within

which they must be received by that department or individual(s).

3. **Tracking or Logging.** Design, implement, and maintain a consistent tracking mechanism for logging and monitoring the receipt of the Communication and the process for handling until the matter is resolved.

4. **Deadline Adherence.** Calendar the deadlines by which responses must be received and set up controls to ensure all responses are sent by their deadlines. Appoint a department or individual(s) with ultimate accountability for ensuring deadlines are met. If additional time is needed to investigate, make sure extensions are requested before deadlines have expired and track all date extensions accordingly.

5. **Response Requirements.** Pay strict attention to the requirements set forth for the response, including content, evidence, form of delivery, and to whom the response should be directed.

6. **Authorized Parties.** Designate the department and/or individual(s) within the company who are authorized to respond to the Communications and ensure no unauthorized parties submit responses without seeking prior written approval.

7. **Investigate.** Conduct an internal investigation into any allegations set forth or information being requested. Determine if an independent third-party investigation is needed or if external counsel should be retained to assist.

   a. Interview any necessary and relevant witnesses in conjunction with the investigation.

   b. Review relevant and applicable documentation, including any audio or video evidence available.

8. **Response.** Draft and prepare a response for final review by the authorized party. Pay attention to what is requested, and be sure to include information responsive to the requests.

9. **Response Delivery**. Once the response is approved by the authorized party, send the response according to the instructions contained within the Communication.

10. **Update Log**. Update the tracking mechanism to show the date the Response was sent, where it was sent, and the delivery method for sending. Continue to update as new developments occur.

11. **Document Retention.** Maintain a copy of the entire file contents, including the original Communication, notes, documentation, and Response, for at least three years from the date the matter is considered closed.

Appendix O: Insurance Coverage Checklist

There are several types of insurance policies a business should consider to limit their liability and exposure in the event of unplanned accidents and incidents and to provide protection against the adverse actions of others. To be sure that your business is protected, review this Appendix checklist for the most common and necessary types of insurance.

General Liability Insurance

General Liability Insurance covers a business for a variety of accidental bodily injuries, property damage, product liability, copyright infringement, and defamation claims.

What types of businesses need this?

- A business with a physical office that invites the public, customers/clients, or vendors onto its premises or to other locations.

- A business that prepares advertising and/or marketing materials.

- A business that uses social media.

- A business that submits bids for, or solicits contracts from, businesses that require general liability insurance.

Employment Practices Liability Insurance (EPLI)

Employment Practices Liability Insurance protects a business from claims made by employees for wrongful acts that occur during employment.

What actions are covered?

- Discrimination (based on sex, race, age, disability, gender, ancestry, national origin, etc.)

- Harassment

- Wrongful termination

- Retaliation

Professional Liability Insurance

Professional Liability Insurance (also known as Error and Omissions Insurance) protects a business from damages due to claims of negligence, errors, omissions, and mistakes made by its employees.

What types of businesses need this?

- Accountants, tax preparers, investment advisors, stockbrokers

- Attorneys

- Architects, engineers

- Health care professionals (i.e., physicians, counselors, dentists, trainers)

- Real estate agents

- Insurance professionals

- Consultants

- Information technology professionals

Commercial Property Insurance

Commercial Property Insurance protects a business from loss due to damages to building premises, owned or leased equipment, and other property damages.

What types of businesses need this?

- A business with a mortgage on a property.

- A business that rents or leases a commercial building, e.g., retail businesses.

- A business with a large investment in leased or owned equipment, e.g., manufacturers.

Directors and Officers Insurance

Directors and Officers Insurance protects a director or an officer of a for-profit or a non-profit company from personal liability, legal fees, and other costs associated with the defense of legal actions brought against them. Generally, fraud and criminal activity are excluded from this type of policy.

Who needs this? Officers or directors who are accused of wrongdoing, such as

- Employment malpractice

- Mismanaged assets or funds

- Disclosure errors

- Reporting errors

- Regulatory violations

- Errors leading to financial loss or bankruptcy

Cyber Liability Insurance

Cyber Liability Insurance is necessary to protect a business from cyber-attacks and interruption of business, causing loss of data, theft of data, loss of revenue, and/or a loss of trust from customers, clients, or employees.

What types of businesses need this? Any business that stores and regularly uses confidential computer data.

Two types of coverage

1. **First-party coverage:** Covers losses and damages incurred by the business itself, including recovering compromised data, lost income, notifying customers or clients of the data breach, regulatory fines, and repairing damaged computer systems.

2. **Third-party coverage:** Covers losses and damages of customers or clients, including credit monitoring, restoring and protecting personal identities, and loss resulting from identity theft.

Commercial Automobile Liability Insurance

Commercial Automobile Liability Insurance protects a business from liability for bodily and personal injury and property damage as a result of an auto accident where the business and/or the employee driver is at fault. Commercial policies usually offer higher limits than personal auto insurance policies.

What types of businesses need this?

- A business that owns, leases, or rents vehicles

- A business that has employees who drive their personal vehicles to conduct business

- A business that has employees that operate leased, rented, or owned company vehicles

What types of businesses need this? Any business that stores and regularly uses confidential computer data.

Two types of coverage

1. **First-party coverage:** Covers losses and damages incurred by the business itself, including recovering compromised data, lost income, notifying customers or clients of the data breach, regulatory fines, and repairing damaged computer systems.

2. **Third-party coverage:** Covers losses and damages of customers or clients, including credit monitoring, restoring and protecting personal identities, and loss resulting from identity theft.

Commercial Automobile Liability Insurance

Commercial Automobile Liability Insurance protects a business from liability for bodily and personal injury and property damage as a result of an auto accident where the business and/or the employee driver is at fault. Commercial policies usually offer higher limits than personal auto insurance policies.

What types of businesses need this?

- A business that owns, leases, or rents vehicles

- A business that has employees who drive their personal vehicles to conduct business

- A business that has employees that operate leased, rented, or owned company vehicles

Appendix P: How to Protect Trade Secrets

In Chapter 5, we discussed the impact competitors can have on your business and the importance of protecting and keeping confidential your trade secrets through the use of restrictive covenants contained within certain contractual agreements between you and your employees. This checklist provides some additional best practices you can use to prevent your competitors from learning your trade secrets.

1. Create agreements, policies, procedures, and records to govern the production of documents to third parties.

   a. Draft nondisclosure agreements ("NDA") for use with prospective vendors, suppliers, and other types of potential business partners (collectively, "Prospects") that include secrecy and nonuse obligations, audit rights, and provisions for post-relationship obligations.

    i. Have both parties execute the NDA prior to entering into negotiations or disclosing any confidential information.

    ii. Pursuing a claim for breach of your NDA can be easier to enforce than attempting to pursue misappropriation of a trade secret.

    iii. Only share proprietary information on a need-to-know basis.

b. For software companies, draft licensing agreements that include nondisclosure and nonuse obligations when providing certain products to customers.

    i. Include digital rights management and robust licensing terms in the customer licensing agreements that contain anti-reverse engineering.

    ii. Require third parties who are provided confidential information to immediately notify you in the event of unauthorized disclosure or dissemination of confidential information and take all available measures to stop any further breaches and to recapture the unauthorized disclosure.

      iii. Confirm the agreement complies with the local privacy laws of where the party is located.

      iv. Include Intellectual Property ownership rights provisions in all terms and conditions.

  c. Ensure the person executing any agreement between your Company and a Prospect is authorized to sign on the Prospect's behalf.

  d. Establish internal written policies and procedures for trade secret management.

2. Establish physical and electronic security and confidentiality measures.

  a. Compartmentalize trade secrets from one another to make them more difficult to copy.

  b. Keep designs or latest-generation technology available only to those who need to know about them.

  c. Classify and mark confidential information according to sensitivity and assign internal and external access accordingly.

  d. Restrict access to databases through passwords and multi-factor authentication.

e. Closely monitor the entry and exit of storage devices, laptops, mobile devices, etc., in secure environments.

f. Track data flows and file transfers.

3. Assess risks to identify and prioritize trade secret vulnerabilities.

a. Designate documents containing confidential information as "confidential."

b. Identify and categorize trade secrets and prioritize resources to protect those with the highest value.

4. Establish due diligence and ongoing third-party vendor/supplier management programs.

a. Carefully select and closely monitor all business partners with access to confidential information.

b. Run background checks on Prospects before beginning negotiations.

c. Conduct comprehensive due diligence before selecting a Prospect.

d. Select business partners that have brand images and reputations of their own and experience protecting their own IP.

e. Manage supplier and vendor relationships through multiple personnel to prevent members from cultivating a comprehensive personal network.

f. Require customers to maintain adequate security systems that will sufficiently protect any sensitive software programs.

g. Only provide customers with access to the programs designed for their particular use.

5. Institute an information protection team and program.

a. Implement policies, procedures, and practices designed to protect trade secrets from unintended disclosure.

6. Training and capacity building with employees and third parties.

a. Educate and train employees on policies and procedures and encourage enforcement as a company-wide effort for which everyone is responsible.

7. Monitor and measure corporate efforts coordinated to protect trade secrets.

a. Feed fictitious compilations of data into databases to easily identify misappropriation.

    b. Place notices on software programs, data displays, accompanying documentation, and manuals warning against disclosure, copying, and other misuse.

8. Take preventative and corrective actions and continually improve policies and procedures.

    a. Secure your trade secrets before exploring business relationships with Prospects.

    b. Keep good records, as enforcement actions will typically require original documentary evidence.

Appendix Q: Exempt Employees Checklist

In Chapter 6, we explained that paying employees a salary is not enough for them to be properly classified as exempt employees. You may be mistakenly paying non-exempt salaried employees on an exempt basis, which means you may be liable for minimum wages and overtime pay to those employees. You may be asking, "If paying a salary is insufficient, then what is?"

Exempt Employees

Employees must satisfy all of the following elements to be considered an exempt employee under the Fair Labor Standards Act:

- Be paid on a salary basis

- The salary must meet or exceed $684 per week

The employee's specific job duties must satisfy one of the following exemption categories:

- Executive

- Administrative

- Professional

- Computer

- Outside sales

Executive Exemption

To satisfy the executive exemption, the employee's job must satisfy the following requirements:

- Primary duties must be managing the enterprise or managing a customarily recognized department or subdivision of the enterprise.

- The employee must customarily and regularly direct the work of at least two or more other full-time employees or their equivalent.

- The employee must have the authority to hire or fire other employees, or the employee's suggestions and recommendations as to the hiring, firing, advancement, promotion, or any other change of status of other employees must be given particular weight.

Administrative Exemption

To satisfy the administrative exemption, the employee's job must satisfy the following requirements:

- The employee's primary duty must be the performance of office or non-manual work directly related to the management or general business operations of the employer or the employer's customers.

- The employee's primary duty includes the exercise of discretion and independent judgment with respect to matters of significance.

When the requirement says "directly related to management or general business operations," that means that the functions performed by the employee must assist with the running or servicing of the business, such as accounting, marketing, and human resources, among others. This would not include employees working production in a manufacturing operation or selling products retail.

Professional Exemption

To satisfy the professional exemption, the employee's job must satisfy the following requirements:

- The employee's primary duty must be the performance of work requiring advanced knowledge, defined as work that is predominantly intellectual in character and which includes work requiring the consistent exercise of discretion and judgment.

- The advanced knowledge must be in a field of science or learning.

- The advanced knowledge must be customarily acquired by a prolonged course of specialized intellectual instruction.

For the purposes of the professional exemption under the Fair Labor Standards Act, the term "fields of science or learning" include the following areas: law, medicine, theology, accounting, actuarial computation, engineering, architecture, teaching, various types of physical, chemical and biological sciences, pharmacy, and other occupations that have a recognized professional status. These professions are distinguished from mechanical arts or skill trades in which the knowledge is advanced, but the field is not science or learning.

Computer Employee Exemption

To satisfy the computer employee exemption, the employee's job must satisfy the following requirements:

- The employee must be employed as a computer systems analyst, computer programmer, software engineer, or other similarly skilled worker in the computer field performing the duties described below.

- The employee's primary duty must consist of any of the following:

  - The application of systems analysis techniques and procedures, including consulting with users, to determine hardware, software, or system functional specifications.

  - The design, development, documentation, analysis, creation, testing, or modification of computer systems or programs, including prototypes, based on and related to user or system design specifications.

  - The design, documentation, testing, creation, or modification of computer programs related to machine operating systems.

  - A combination of the aforementioned duties, the performance of which requires the same level of skills.

It is important to note that this exemption does not include employees who manufacture or repair computer hardware and equipment.

Outside Sales Exemption

To satisfy the outside sales exemption, the employee's job must satisfy the following requirements:

- The employee's primary duty must be making sales (as defined in the FLSA) or obtaining orders or contracts for services or for the use of facilities for which a consideration will be paid by the client or customer.

- The employee must be customarily and regularly engaged away from the employer's place or places of business.

The salary required does not apply to the outside sales exemption; thus, you can classify outside sales personnel who are not paid on a salary basis as exempt employees. For the purposes of the outside sales exemption of the Fair Labor Standards Act, the term "sales" in the "making sales" requirement refers to any sale, exchange, contract to sell, consignment for sales, shipment for sale, or other disposition, as well as the transfer of title to tangible property, and in certain cases, of tangible and valuable evidences of intangible property. An outside sales employee does not need to be away from your business's main operation 100% of the time. As long as the outside sales employee is away from your places of business as a normal part of the employee's workweek, that will satisfy the "customarily and regularly" requirement.

Primary Duty

Throughout these exemptions, the focus is on the employee's "primary duty." The critical aspect here is that the employee's job description and actual job performance must center on the executive, administrative, professional, computer, or outside sales functions, as discussed above. Primary duty means the principal, main, major, or most important duty that the employee performs. Determination of an employee's primary duty must be based on all the facts in a particular case, with a major emphasis on the character of the employee's job as a whole.

Discretion and Independent Judgment

In general, the exercise of discretion and independent judgment involves the comparison and evaluation of possible courses of conduct and acting or making a decision after the various possibilities have been considered. The term must be applied in light of all the facts involved in the employee's particular employment situation and implies that the employee has the authority to make an independent choice, free from immediate direction or supervision. Factors to consider include, but are not limited to, whether the employee

- Has the authority to formulate, affect, interpret, or implement management policies or operating practices

- Carries out major assignments in conducting the operations of the business

- Performs work that affects business operations to a substantial degree

- Has the authority to commit the employer in matters that have a significant financial impact

- Has the authority to waive or deviate from established policies and procedures without prior approval and other factors set forth in the regulation

The fact that an employee's decisions are revised or reversed after review does not mean that the employee is not exercising discretion and independent judgment. The exercise of discretion and independent judgment must be more than the use of skill in applying well-established techniques, procedures, or specific standards described in manuals or other sources.

Matters of Significance

The term "matters of significance" refers to the level of importance or consequence of the work performed. An employee does not exercise discretion and independent judgment with respect to matters of significance merely because the employer will experience financial losses if the employee fails to perform the job properly. Similarly, an employee who operates expensive equipment does not exercise discretion and independent judgment with respect to matters of significance merely because improper performance of the employee's duties may cause serious financial loss to the employer.

Work Requiring Advanced Knowledge

For the learned professional exemption, the employee must perform work requiring "advanced knowledge" in a "field of science or learning." Advanced knowledge means work that is predominantly intellectual in nature and requires the consistent exercise of discretion and judgment. Fields of science and learning include law, medicine, accounting, engineering, physical, chemical, or biological sciences, pharmacy, and other occupations having a recognized professional status. These fields are distinguished from skilled trades that may require advanced knowledge but are not considered a field of science or learning.

Appendix R: Employees versus Independent Contractors

In Chapter 6, we discussed an issue plaguing many businesses, which is misclassifying employees as independent contractors. If you misclassify employees as independent contractors, the employee may have wage and hour claims against you to the extent that the fees paid to the employee fall below the minimum in relation to the hours worked or the hours worked by the employee entitled the employee to overtime. Further, if you were not satisfied with the requirement for withholding income and payroll taxes, you may be liable for those taxes plus a penalty.

These are only a few of the issues that you can encounter from misclassification. The consequences of misclassification can be dire, so making sure you are getting the classification correct should be an ongoing process between you and your attorney. You should use this appendix as a checklist to make sure that you and your attorney are analyzing all the factors that courts and agencies consider in the employee versus independent contractor analysis.

General Factors

Courts apply the following general factors for deciding who has the right to control the manner and means of doing the work:

1. Who controls the details and quality of work.

2. Who controls the hours worked.

3. Who selects the materials, tools, and personnel used.

4. Who selects the routes traveled.

5. Length of employment.

6. Type of business.

7. Method of payment.

8. Any pertinent agreements or contracts.

Remember that the contract language between you and the worker does not determine the worker's classification as an employee and independent contractor. It is only one factor of many. Courts and governmental agencies will always look to the objective nature of the relationship by analyzing the totality of the facts and circumstances. In general, the central idea behind the independent contractor versus employee analysis is the extent of control that you possess over the manner and means of doing the worker's work.

Unemployment Compensation

Courts and governmental agencies have used a more expansive list of factors when analyzing whether a worker is an employee or independent contractor regarding unemployment compensation. The factors that these courts and agencies use are:

- The worker is required to comply with the instructions of the person for whom services are being performed regarding when, where, and how the worker is to perform the services.

- The person for whom services are being performed requires particular training for the worker performing services.

- The services provided are part of the regular business of the person from whom services are being performed.

- The person for whom services are being performed requires that services be provided by a particular worker.

- The person for whom services are being performed hires, supervises, or pays the wages of the worker performing services.

- A continuing relationship exists between the person for whom services are being performed and the worker performing services that contemplates continuing or recurring work, even if not full-time.

- The person for whom services are being performed requires set hours during which services are to be performed.

- The person for whom services are being performed requires the worker to devote himself or herself full-time to the business of the person for whom services are being performed.

- The person for whom services are being performed requires that work be performed on its premises.

- The person for whom services are being performed requires that the worker follow the order of work set by the person for whom services are being performed.

- The person for whom services are being performed requires the worker to make oral or written progress reports.

- The person for whom services are being performed pays the worker on a regular basis, such as hourly, weekly, or monthly.

- The person for whom services are being performed pays expenses for the worker performing services.

- The person for whom services are being performed furnishes tools, instrumentalities, and other materials for use by the worker in performing services.

- There is a lack of investment by the worker in the facilities used to perform services.

- There is a lack of profit or loss to the worker performing services because of the performance of such services.

- The worker performing services is not performing services for several persons at the same time.

- The worker performing services does not make such services available to the public.

- The person for whom services are being performed has a right to discharge the worker performing services.

- The worker performing services has the right to end the relationship with the person for whom services are being performed without incurring liability pursuant to an employment contract or agreement.

Many of these factors overlap with the eight or so factors that courts typically use, as discussed above. Make sure to periodically review the relationship you have with all independent contractors that you have engaged to determine whether you need to classify them as an employee going forward and whether you need to take any action to remedy any labor and tax law issues that may arise from the worker being an employee.

Appendix S: FMLA Compliance Checklist

In Chapter 6, we discussed many laws governing the relationship between employers and employees, including the Family and Medical Leave Act. Under the Family and Medical Leave Act, eligible employees of covered employers are entitled to take unpaid, job-protected leaves of absence for certain family and medical reasons with guaranteed continuation of group health insurance coverage. This Appendix will assist you with FMLA compliance.

Is Your Company Required to Comply with FMLA?

Your company is required to comply with FMLA if it has fifty or more employees on its payroll for a total of at least twenty total workweeks, either this year or the previous year.

An employer that satisfies the preceding criteria is a "covered employer." For example, if your company employed sixty employees on its payroll last year for only ten workweeks, and all other workweeks employed only forty-five employees, your company would not be required to comply with FMLA. However, if you employed seventy employees last year for the entire year but, due to financial issues, are only employing forty employees this year, your business is still required to comply with FMLA.

Is the Employee Requesting FMLA Leave Eligible?

An employee is eligible to take FMLA leave if *all three* of the following elements are satisfied.

- The employee has been employed by you for a total of twelve months (these twelve months do not need to be consecutive).

- The employee has worked at least 1,250 hours over the twelve months preceding the requested leave.

- the employee works at a location that has at least 50 employees living within a 75-mile radius of the location.

  - Keep in mind that if the number of employees living within a 75-mile radius of the location falls below 50, employees remain eligible for one year after the number of employees within 75 miles falls below 50.

For example, if you had a location that employed 55 employees living within 75 miles of that location until March

31, 2022, at which time the number of employees within 75 miles fell to 48 employees, then the employee requesting leave is still eligible under this element until March 31, 2023.

What Reasons Qualify under the FMLA for Leave?

Your company must grant FMLA leave of up to 12 work-weeks in a 12-month period to an eligible employee for any of the following reasons:

- A serious health condition is affecting the employee, which makes the employee unable to work.

- A spouse, child, or parent is suffering from a serious health condition.

- The employee or the employee's spouse birthed a child, or the employee received placement of a child for adoption or foster care.

- Military leave, including leave related to the employee's spouse, child, or parent being on active duty in a foreign country or is called to active duty status in a foreign country (or is notified of an imminent call to active duty).

- To care for a spouse, child, parent, or next-of-kin servicemember receiving medical treatment for a serious health condition or has been placed on the temporary disability retired list for a serious health condition.

- Other military leave reasons stated in 29 C.F.R. § 825.126.

An eligible employee may take multiple FMLA absences for the same reason, and the absences will be considered a single leave.

What Is a Serious Health Condition?

The FMLA defines a serious health condition as an illness, injury, impairment, or physical or mental condition that involves inpatient care in a hospital, hospice, or residential medical care facility or continuing treatment by a health care provider.

Your company cannot require an employee unable to work due to serious health problems to accept a light-duty assignment.

Appendix T: Restrictive Covenants Checklist

In Chapter 5, we addressed how Restrictive Covenants are significant tools to protect a business's value and investments in confidential information, trade secrets, and employee training. The following is a checklist of important considerations for determining the need of the business for the different types of restrictive covenants that can be used and what should be contained in those covenants and agreements.

Employee Non-Compete and Non-Solicitation Covenants/Agreements

1. **Define business interests** the employer is seeking to protect.

2. **Identify who has access** to the confidential information and why it needs to be protected.

3. **Specify the consideration** provided to the employee and acknowledgment from the employee that they are receiving adequate consideration and

that restrictions are needed to protect legitimate business interests.

4. **Identify what the non-compete intends to protect** from unauthorized competitive use.

5. **Define non-compete restrictions post-employment**

    a. Specify competitors; any competitor or certain named competitors

    b. Specify the particular geographic area

    c. Specify the given role in the employer's industry

    d. Include a time period limitation

6. **Define parameters of non-solicitation on the following**

    a. All Employer's customers

    b. Employer's customers serviced by employee

    c. Customers or prospective customers solicited, serviced, or contacted by employee

    d. Current employees

    e. All employees who left the employer within a defined time before the employee's departure

    f. Include a time period limitation

7. **Establish a social media conduct policy**. Subject to rights provided by Section 7, National Labor Relations Act (NLRA).

8. **Include choice of law** and forum selection provisions.

9. **Consider non-disparagement provisions**. Subject to rights provided by Section 7, NLRA.

10. **Add a tolling provision** to suspend the restrictive period during times when the employee is violating the contract during litigation.

11. **Include notice of immunities** available under the Defend Trade Secrets Act (DTSA).

Employee Confidentiality and Non-Disclosure Covenants/Agreements

1. **Define with specificity the confidential information** being protected.

2. **Identify information qualified as a trade secret** under applicable state law and include an acknowledgment from the employee of the information's status as a trade secret.

3. **Exclude employee wages and benefits** information to avoid NLRA violations.

4. **Include a disclaimer** that the agreement does not

prevent the employee from exercising Section 7 rights under NLRA.

5. **Exclude certain activities protected by law and public policy,** such as disclosure of corporate wrongdoing to government agencies, sexual harassment, or other discrimination claims.

6. **Include specific examples** tailored to the particular business and industry.

7. **Include various formats** information could be in.

8. **Define employee's obligations** under the agreement.

9. **Specify procedures** the employee must follow before disclosing information when permitted.

10. **Identify internal steps and protections** the employee must take to protect confidential information from inappropriate use or disclosure.

11. **Include notice of immunities** available under the DTSA.

12. **Identify the harm or injury** the employer would suffer as a result of disclosure of the confidential information.

13. **Clearly state that confidentiality obligations survive termination** of the employment relationship.

14. **Require the employee to return all confidential information** in the employee's possession immediately upon termination of employment.

15. **Address IP ownership** if appropriate.

16. **Include injunctive relief** as a remedy in the event of a breach.

Notes

1. National Small Business Association. "2018 Small Business Taxation Survey," 2018. https://www.nsba.biz/_files/ugd/fec11a_ebbe373bb0694a2b94ee17155258200c.pdf.

2. Kathryn Rubino, "Biglaw Firms Have Too Many Lawyers with Attorney Productivity at an Historic Low," Above the Law, August 22, 2023, https://abovethelaw.com/2023/08/biglaw-firms-have-too-many-lawyers-with-attorney-productivity-at-an-historic-low/ .

3. Lawyers for Civil Justice et al. "Litigation Cost Survey of Major Companies." Duke Law School, 2010 Conference on Civil Litigation, May 10-11, 2010. https://www.uscourts.gov/sites/default/files/litigation_cost_survey_of_major_companies_0.pdf , Accessed March 15, 2023. Above amounts are adjusted for inflation.

4. Note that there are nuanced, technical exceptions, as in scenarios with injured parties who are not in contract with those being sued. Examples are neighbors, subrogation plaintiffs, contractual assignees, innocent bystanders, and traffic accident victims. The CoverMySix method still applies to protect the business from these plaintiffs, however, because it covers their risk in the employee and customer categories. In other words, treating each of these potential plaintiffs as customers, and solid employment policies and practices, will protect the business from these plaintiffs. Further, the CoverMySix method requires the business to re-evaluate its insurance coverage, which (as will be further explained below) may be expanded to protect the business from each of the above outliers as well.

5. Lovitt & Touchè, "Risky Business: Right-Size Your Insurance to Save Money, Protect Assets," *Phoenix Business Journal*, February 22, 2019. https://www.bizjournals.com/phoenix/news/2019/02/22/risky-business-right-size-your-insurance-to-save.html .

6. It costs approximately $70,484 to litigate a premises liability claim, adjusted for inflation. Paula Hannaford-Agor, "Measuring the Cost of Civil Litigation: Findings from a Survey of Trial Lawyers," *Voir Dire* 22, (Spring 2013): 22–28, https://ncsc.contentdm.oclc.org .

7. The three types of people who may be on a property are invitees, licensees, and trespassers. Invitees are invited onto the property to conduct business, such as customers in a store. Property owners owe them a duty to maintain a safe environment and to warn them of any potential hazards that are not obvious. Licensees are on the property with the owner's consent but for their own purposes, such as social guests. Property owners have a duty to warn them of known hazards that the licensee is unlikely to discover. Trespassers are on the property without the owner's consent. Property owners have a limited duty to trespassers, typically requiring the owner to not intentionally harm the trespasser. In some circumstances, such as when children are involved, the property owner may have a higher duty of care.

8. Federal Trade Commission. "Penalty Offenses Concerning Substantiation." April 13, 2023, https://www.ftc.gov/enforcement/notices-penalty -offenses/penalty-offenses-concerning-substantiation .

9. "International Association for Contract and Commercial Management," IACCM, accessed March 24, 2023, https://www.iaccm.com/resources/? id=10623.

10. In most states, this would not be considered the unlicensed practice of law. But laws, advisory opinions, and regulations change, so have this vetted by counsel. Your business lawyer should confirm that your employee may use the playbook without such risk.

11. https://www.supremecourt.gov/opinions/17pdf/17-494_j4el.pdf https://plus.lexis.com/document?pdmfid=1530671&pddocfullpath=%2Fsh ared%2Fdocument%2Fcases%2Furn%3AcontentItem%3A686R-PBV1-D Y89-M3NM-00000-00&pdcontentcomponentid=6443&prid=a8cdb67f -250f-4455-8688-f4065e21ff5c&crid=f8ac9da7-5bb6-44a7-b964-c1517a 47bd36&pdisdocsliderrequired=true&pdpeersearchid=8b0ef39b-b5ee-4 8d9-80a3-882672ca3db9-1&ecomp=_7tgk&earg=pdsf .

12. Christine Lacagnina, "Employment Practices Liability Insurance: Match with a Local Agent," TrustedChoice.com, October 6, 2023, https://www .trustedchoice.com/business-insurance/liability/epli/ .

13. Patrick Mitchell, "The 2017 Hiscox Guide to Employee Lawsuits," (2017), https://www.hiscox.com/documents/2017-Hiscox-Guide-to-Em ployee-Lawsuits.pdf?State=NC .

14. US Equal Employment Opportunity Commission, "Remedies for Employment Discrimination,", accessed March 2, 2023, https://www.eeoc.gov/remedies-employment-discrimination#:~:text=Re medies%20May%20Include%20Compensatory%20%26%20Punitive,%2 C%20disability%2C%20or%20genetic%20information .

15. Occupational Safety and Health Administration, " Top 10 Most Frequently Cited Standards," accessed March 24, 2023, https://www.osha.gov/to p10citedstandards .

16. Occupational Safety and Health Administration, " 2023 Annual Adjustments to OSHA Civil Penalties," accessed March 24, 2023, https://www.osha.gov/memos/2022-12-20/2023-annual-adjustm ents-osha-civil-penalties .

17. Legal Information Institute, "29 U.S. Code § 216 - Penalties," accessed March 24, 2023, https://www.law.cornell.edu/uscode/text/29/216 .

18. We want to again reiterate the fact that in 95% of cases, plaintiffs can be easily categorized in six ways, a seventh plaintiff can emerge in a minority of cases in the area of employees. These situations deal with outlier occurrences where someone who is not under contract with the one being sued has a claim for damages for harm done. These situations can be covered by good insurance and the concepts found in this chapter.

19. An Ishikawa diagram, also known as a "Fishbone Diagram," is a cause analysis tool that assists problem solvers with brainstorming causes and potential contributing factors to a problem or effect. To create an Ishikawa diagram, draw an arrow like the example diagram shown. At the head of the diagram, write down the problem you are trying to solve. At the end of the branching lines, write down the categories of potential causes, such as "manpower," "methods," "environment," etc. Brainstorm potential causes of the problem with your team and write them down under the applicable category. Next, brainstorm solutions to improve the causes of the problem and assign the highest impact, easiest implementation solutions to team members to execute. Using a brainstorming method like this will help you and your team effectively troubleshoot and solve problems that could pose a legal threat to your business.

Acknowledgments

We stand on the shoulders of giants.

Ordinarily, that phrase is used to describe ancestors and historical icons, but in this case, it befits our team at Gertsburg Licata and CoverMySix. They are the hardest-working and most talented teammates we could ever want. Nothing about this book or the CoverMySix system would be possible without their tireless effort and enduring support. We built our organization with their sweat, and for a million other reasons, we love them.

We especially thank Cassie Pinkerton, Max Julian, Gene Friedman, Randi Nine, and Michael Beardsley for their hands-on work on this book and the CoverMySix system.

In addition to our amazing employees, we thank our advisory board members—Kris Snyder, Gabe Torok, and Paul Chaffee, and the countless clients and business partners who have supported the evolution of CoverMySix over the years.

And, of course, none of this would be even remotely possible without Linna and Tiffany, our truly better halves.

Thank you all for Covering our Sixes so well.

About the Authors

 **Alex Gertsburg** is a co-managing Partner of Gertsburg Licata and CEO of CoverMySix, LLC. He has over 20 years of experience as a global litigator and deal lawyer.

Mr. Gertsburg also proudly served in Iraq as a combat convoy commander, serving in reserve and active-duty roles with the US Army for ten years. He then became the first General Counsel for Broadvox in 2006, where he served for ten years and led the company's legal department through numerous and varied legal matters before starting his law firm and co-founding CoverMySix.

Outside of law, Mr. Gertsburg enjoys his family, traveling, mentoring entrepreneurs, hiking, history, and his Harley V-Rod.

 **Lou Licata** is a co-managing Partner of Gertsburg Licata Co., LPA, and co-founder of CoverMySix, LLC. He is responsible for the management of the firm's legal operations and oversight of its various practice areas, including the Global Business Group. He focuses his practice on serving as Chief Legal Advisor to CEOs and business owners throughout the world.

Mr. Licata has received an "A" peer-review rating, the highest acknowledgment possible in his profession, from Martindale Hubbell. He was also the first attorney in the State of Ohio certified as a dual specialist and was recognized as a "Super Lawyer" by *Ohio Lawyer Magazine.*

Mr. Licata has been a leader in the profession, starting one of the first internet law practices in the United States and implementing innovative firm management measures, including a paperless office initiative in 1998.

In the business community, Mr. Licata served on the Global Board of Directors for the Entrepreneur's Organization and was the former Chairman of The Council of Small Enterprises.

CONNECT WITH US

Follow us on your favorite social media platforms today.

Stay up to date. Don't miss weekly posts and videos from Alex and Lou with tips to keep your company lawsuit free.

CoverMySix.com/Blog

About CoverMySix®

W E'VE CHANGED THE WAY businesses work with attorneys. CoverMySix is an innovative anti-litigation solution service that revolutionizes the approach to risk mitigation and legal protection for business owners. Our mission is to create freedom and growth for entrepreneurs and their ventures by providing a proactive and systematic solution to illuminate potential litigation risks.

With CoverMySix, business owners can establish worry-free operations, whether they are launching a new venture or expanding an existing one. Our team of experienced professionals is dedicated to identifying and neutralizing litigation and investigation hazards for businesses of all sizes. We understand that every business is unique, but through our vast experience in handling thousands of business matters and litigating hundreds of lawsuits, we have identified the six types of plaintiffs that can pose legal challenges: customers, competitors, employees, owners/shareholders, vendors/suppliers, and government.

At CoverMySix, we offer a novel approach to business operations and compliance that gives owners and CEOs the peace of mind to focus on driving innovation and growth.

Our name, CoverMySix, is derived from military terminology, referring to the six o'clock position on a clock, which means "watch my back." We believe the best way for attorneys to support businesses is by proactively identifying and addressing issues before they arise, ensuring that potential legal headaches are knocked out.

Trust CoverMySix to protect your business from legal risks and safeguard your path to success. Discover more at Co verMySix.com

About Our Law Firm

Gertsburg Licata Co., LPA is a dynamic global business law firm with an unwavering commitment to protecting and growing our business clients' interests. Led by experienced attorneys and business owners Louis J. Licata and Alex Gertsburg, we bring decades of expertise in working with our clients to develop and execute successful business strategies. At Gertsburg Licata, we provide practical solutions to companies at every stage of growth. We are lawyers by trade and entrepreneurs by nature.

We understand that our clients' businesses represent a significant investment of time, talent, passion, and financial resources. That's why we work closely with them to identify proactive and innovative business transactions and implement aggressive litigation strategies when necessary. Our team is a coalition of business owners, corporate attorneys, and former in-house counsel, offering a well-rounded perspective on the multitude of issues our clients face as business owners and operators. Our core areas of expertise include contract analysis and negotiation, business formation, corporate governance, business dispute litigation, mergers & acquisitions, financing, real estate law, and navigating domestic and global markets.

OUR MISSION is to create freedom and growth for entrepreneurs and their ventures. We believe freedom is both a journey and a destination, and growth is the vehicle that gets you there. At Gertsburg Licata, we serve as your compass, helping you navigate the complex legal and regulatory landscape that every entrepreneur and business leader encounters. Based in Cleveland, we proudly serve clients from around the globe. Whether your company is headquartered in Ohio or anywhere else in the United States, our experienced business attorneys are ready to assist you with transactional and litigation matters of any size, in any industry, and in any location.

Visit our website at GertsburgLicata.com

KEYNOTE SPEAKER

MULTIPLE BREAKTHROUGH TOPICS

Let Alex teach you and your team how to negotiate, tackle your obstacles effectively, and build a Lawsuit-Free Company.

START THE
CONVERSATION TODAY

CoverMySix.com/Alex

THIS BOOK IS PROTECTED INTELLECTUAL PROPERTY

The author of this book values Intellectual Property. The book you just read is protected by Easy IP™, a proprietary process, which integrates blockchain technology giving Intellectual Property "Global Protection." By creating a "Time-Stamped" smart contract that can never be tampered with or changed, we establish "First Use" that tracks back to the author.

Easy IP™ functions much like a Pre-Patent™ since it provides an immutable "First Use" of the Intellectual Property. This is achieved through our proprietary process of leveraging blockchain technology and smart contracts. As a result, proving "First Use" is simple through a global and verifiable smart contract. By protecting intellectual property with blockchain technology and smart contracts, we establish a "First to File" event.

Powered By Easy IP™

LEARN MORE AT EASYIP.TODAY

Made in the USA
Monee, IL
22 January 2024

51726046R00174